DREAMS & JEALOUSY

The Story of Holocaust Survivor Jack Repp

DREAMS & JEALOUSY

The Story of Holocaust Survivor Jack Repp

AS TOLD TO DAN LEWIN

WRITTEN WELLSPRINGS, LLC

This book is dedicated to my parents, Lazer and Chava Rzepkowicz.
It's been 80 years since I last saw them,
yet not a day goes by that they aren't on my mind and in my speech.
May their memory be a blessing!

Copyright © 2017 by Written Wellsprings, LLC
Cover design by Chrystina Cleveland · Typesetting by Bernstein Graphics

Contents

Introduction

I first met Jack Repp after my wife pushed me to attend a lecture at the local Jewish Federation, advertised as a Holocaust survivor's testimony. Going in, I wasn't keen on hearing another Holocaust lecture. I figured I had already absorbed my fair share of these speeches over the years. And how much can a person really take away from listening to accounts of tragedies?

But this lecture caught me by surprise—it had a different vibe. It seemed to me that, for a change, the words weren't scripted; the speaker wasn't trying to inspire or move his audience, nor was he diplomatic. It was raw and real. At times I could feel a thick intensity in the room as I watched members of the audience sitting there uncomfortable but captivated, stunned by the stories they were hearing. More to the point, I was drawn to Jack's physical and emotional strength. He had a certain power and fearlessness, and at the same moment a sweetness and sensitivity.

After the lecture, I approached Jack and asked about the specific work he did with the United States intelligence service hunting Nazis, along with a few other questions. During our brief exchange he said, "You know, in these lectures, I relate only a fraction of the things I witnessed."

Acknowledging that a one-hour lecture provides only a glimpse, I inquired whether he'd ever considered putting together a more complete version in a book. He said that over the years people had often mentioned the idea to him, but the timing was never right. I told him that I had helped several members in the community to create their memoirs and suggested that perhaps he'd be interested in working together. "Let's do it!" he answered.

Over the course of the next year, we met at his house once a week for a few hours at a time. We just talked. The more I heard, the more important I found it to capture and preserve this vital material—before it disappeared from the next generation.

In general, the atrocities of the Nazis against Jews have a unique place in history due to their sheer cold-blooded organization and the systematic, long-term sustainability of the horror. Recording the personal stories of those who survived, and who fought, is especially important.

I've heard complaints that the events surrounding the Holocaust have, in a way, been overexposed. When a person walks through a museum, for example, or watches a documentary, there is a natural barrier and limit to how much someone can internalize. The visitor is bombarded with horrific black-and-white footage, images of emaciated prisoners in camps, skeletons being tossed into mass graves. Together with the visual overload comes a ton of statistics and historical facts about the war. And so it becomes difficult to appreciate the true impact on people's lives—everything remains removed from our experience. *Oh, how terrible*, you think, before walking out the door and snapping back into your modern luxurious existence.

In contrast, a memoir evokes imagination and identification. You take the journey with a survivor, gain insight into the background of his hometown, get to know the personalities of his parents, and most of all appreciate the tremendous test of faith and character that it must have taken to recover from such devastating loss and to have to start everything anew.

Enthusiastic as I was to undertake this project, I was not prepared for its challenges. In the past, I've assisted entrepreneurs, art collectors, and musicians in creating their memoirs; this was a totally different encounter. As often happens, during good conversations, memories that had been put aside for ages suddenly resurface. But these memories were at times awful, unbearable to hear. As a writer, I had to be disciplined emotionally, knowing when to set aside my feelings and just listen—and when to continue inquiring, digging deeper into what he was thinking and experiencing while it was happening.

Fortunately, I was speaking with a uniquely tough individual—a survivor willing to share so much, ready to answer any question I had. It's also rare to find somebody in his 90s who has the memory, the time, and the energy to give what it takes to produce a fine memoir. Jack had all that, which made the journey toward creating his book much smoother.

In putting this book together, we never aimed to write a long, overarching Holocaust diary, a catalogue of dry facts, or even a life overview. Instead the goal was to deliver a series of sketches from Jack's life, reflections of trials and triumphs—and to do it in the manner that Jack perceived them. Therefore, these collected memoirs are written simply as they were related to me. (Some names have been changed to protect privacy.) Whether they are taken as factual history or as viewed through the prism of memory—stories tend to change shape over time, some acquiring additional sharp edges, others softening over the decades—there is still plenty to be learned from these accounts.

Four main stages appear in this story: Jack's early years before the war, the atrocities of the war, his recovery in Germany and work with the United States intelligence service, and finally moving to Texas to create a new life. This latter journey—life after so much death, social survival after physical survival — is far more difficult than most realize.

I feel privileged to have been able to do my small part in preserving this story. Looking back, I am most proud of the friendship that Jack and I formed.

My thanks to the U.S.C. Shoah Foundation for its visual history archive containing some of Jack's testimony. Arthur Jones provided me with some valuable stories about Jack's effect on the community in South Dallas. Illustrations and cover design were done by Chrystina Cleveland. John Bernstein put together the interior layout. Phyllis DeBlanche, as usual, did a spectacular job of editing and proofreading.

None of this would have been possible without Sarah Yarrin. Her inexhaustible commitment to helping Jack is a thing of beauty. She coordinated every meeting we had, sat there and listened patiently for hours on end, and went through the manuscript with him. She is a truly amazing lady.

There are striking elements to me in the story of any survivor: the auspicious circumstances that led to near-death escapes ("*mazel*," as we say in Hebrew), combined with the person's ingenuity and tremendous inner strength. With Jack, I was also struck by how he wisely and courageously persevered through all aspects of his entire life. It is an honor to have borne witness to his story.

— Dan Lewin, July 2017

Foreword

I am grateful. Six million—men, women, and children—were murdered, for no reason but they were Jewish. I survived. Yet the atrocities I have seen in my life are beyond human comprehension.

In 1949, I arrived in Greenville, Texas, with my wife and baby daughter, to begin a new life in America. For us, as for all survivors, the end of the war was only the start of a daunting new journey. We needed to adapt to living with the scars of loss and the recollections that we'd continue to carry. Every place I turned, there was always something—objects and sounds—that triggered flashbacks of the camps.

I've had plenty of restless nights' sleep over the years, and conversations where I sat with my wife, bitterly reflecting—"Why did such things happen to us?" Of course, there were no answers.

But during those years, my mind was focused on one thing: that my family be treated equally and live the same way that others around them did. Seven days a week, I worked at my store in South Dallas, from early in the morning to late at night, without taking a vacation. Determined to create a normal existence for my family, I buried the horrors of the war; I never wanted my children to grow up hearing stories about concentration camps. The years passed, and I kept quiet.

It was only after meeting my companion, Sarah Yarrin, in 1998 that I started speaking at schools, synagogues, churches, and other venues to share my story. I never accepted a fee for speaking—how could I capitalize on the murder of my family and so many others? I wanted only to go into the room with a clear mind and conscience, to do my part to ensure that what happened would not be forgotten. And that's what I've devoted the last two decades of my life to doing.

Whenever I talked I spoke bluntly and from the heart. At this point, I can talk about anything, not because I am numb — on the contrary, I relive the experiences each time I talk — but because I believe in the importance of my message. Over the years, I've received hundreds of letters from members of the audience. And as I talk, when I look at the expressions on people's faces, I know that what I'm saying is affecting them, that when they return home, or sit down to eat dinner, these stories will be the topic of conversation.

At the conclusion of the talk at these events, I was often approached and asked, "Do you have a book?" and "Would you like to write your memoir?"

"Are you looking to profit from this book?" I would ask. When the answer was "yes," I immediately declined.

But when I met Rabbi Dan Lewin, we connected right from the start. I decided, at the ripe age of 93, to undertake with him the task of putting my story on paper. I'm grateful to G-d that I was not left blank — I haven't forgotten anything — and that I still possess the stamina to sit down and review my life, though I might need a minute to recall some details.

I'm so thankful to Dan for taking on this project and making sure that the complete story will finally be told. I consider this involvement in preserving history to be one of the biggest good deeds that a person can do. My desire is that what happened to me should never happen again to anybody. And if through this book, I can inspire one person to live a better life, then all the time and effort will have been worth it.

— Jack Repp, July 2017

You shall say to your son,
"We were slaves to Pharaoh in Egypt,
and the Lord took us out of Egypt with
a strong hand."

— Deuteronomy 6:21

CHAPTER 1
A Wholesome Existence

I wasn't always Jack Repp. I was born Itzik Rzepkowicz in Radom, Poland, on August 16, 1923, the fourth of five children. The firstborn, my sister, Nacha, was fourteen years older than me. She was just an infant when my parents moved from Końskie to settle in Radom. My oldest brother, Sruel, was ten years older than me; my brother Dovid was two years older than me, and my youngest brother, Yankele, was nine years younger. We lived in a three-bedroom apartment at 4 Mila Street.

My father, Lazer, worked as a moneylender and had a range of customers, from the tailor who needed to borrow money for materials, to a man looking to open a business. Other individuals pawned their nicest jewelry. Even the guards from the nearby prison occasionally stopped by our house to borrow a few bucks.

My father also made money by cashing checks. The main bank in Radom closed early in the afternoon. But if someone got paid at the close of the workday, where was he to go? So my father figured that if he got a little more cash together and started cashing checks, he could make a good profit. After the local banks closed in the afternoon, he became the bank. He made a nice living and was widely connected.

Busy as he was, my father spent a lot of time at home with his family. He was a tall, lean man, clean shaven with a high and narrow moustache, trimmed so that its width did not extend beyond the sides of his nose. He dressed modern, in a slim suit and a tie, and outside of the synagogue he did not wear a yarmulke. But he was a man of profound faith—not crazy, but committed. Our house had only kosher food. He always closed his business early Friday, in time to prepare for the Sabbath, and he never worked on the seventh day.

The first thing my father did in the morning was to put on his *tallit* (prayer shawl) and *tefilin*. Only then did he sit down to eat. The nearby bakery was owned by a man to whom my father had lent money. Mendel the baker knew what pastries my father liked, and every morning he made a fresh batch especially for him—bagels and braided bread rolls seasoned with salt, pepper, and poppy seeds—and sent it to our house. My father would eat his breakfast rolls with a box of Norwegian sardines and a steaming cup of coffee.

There was no running water. A hired water carrier arrived every so often at our doorstep to deliver big buckets of water for our cistern. We didn't own a car, or even a horse buggy—we went everywhere on foot—but it was a happy, wholesome existence. My parents' biggest pleasure in life was spending time with their children.

The earliest memory I have, from the age of 3, is waking every morning to the sound of my mother singing *"modeh ani lefanecha"* (the Hebrew prayer of gratitude for restoring one's soul each day). As part of the Jewish ritual of washing hands immediately upon awakening, she'd lean down next to my bed, holding a washing cup and large bowl, and rinse my hands, spilling the water into the bowl underneath. My mother always made sure her children were dressed beautifully.

My mother's mother, Raizel Dennenbaum — "the Bobbe Raizel," as we called her — lived nearby and was always at our house. She came from an observant Jewish family, and she covered her hair with the traditional *sheitel*. Her husband, my grandfather Yaakov, was a *Ger Hasid*. He devoted all his time to prayer and the study of Torah while my grandmother went door to door selling clothes. Sadly, he passed away as a young man, and my grandmother raised three daughters alone.

In physical stature, the Bobbe Raziel was a little lady — but an imposing character with an energetic presence. I often remark that she was so resilient, she somehow would have made it well past a hundred years old (if not for the bitter circumstances that took her life). She owned a sweets factory where they made hard candies, and she had several employees. For whatever reason — perhaps to keep her affairs more private — she only hired non-Jewish women, those outside our community. Some of these women had been working for her for 10 or 15 years.

Now, anyone who came to work for the Bobbe Raizel, including me and my brothers, worked hard and got paid well. She also made sure that all her employees sampled the different candies while working — all day long. When it came time to leave, the people were ready to vomit at the sight of candy. "One thing is certain," she used to tell us, "nobody who works in my factory is ever going to steal."

In 1931, a young man named Moshe Golebiowski arrived in Radom to visit his parents, who were our neighbors. They had five older daughters and owned a meat market in the Jewish

My maternal grandfather, Jakob (Yaakov) Dennenbaum.

Dovid (left), my mother, my father, and me.

My grandmother Raizel and me.

quarter. Moshe had been living in Paris for the past seven years, where he worked for his uncle in the 18th arrondissement. He was a handsome fellow with wavy brown hair and light blue eyes, and he was dressed in the latest Parisian fashions—pinstriped suits, bow ties, matching pocket squares, handkerchiefs, and all. During that visit, he and my sister, Nacha, were introduced, and immediately fell in love. "You have the style of a young French lady," he told her. Nacha was captured by his sophistication and elegance, and the promise of a fresh start in Paris. Moshe had little time to waste as his visa was expiring in three months, so he went to ask my father for her hand.

My parents agreed and proceeded to pour all their love, and plenty of resources, into providing their only daughter with the most prestigious event they could. Moshe donned a tuxedo, my sister a gorgeously fashioned white dress. The marriage ceremony was performed under a traditional Jewish chuppah, followed by beautiful festivities complete with a hired band. Family and guests showered the couple with blessings and prayers for a happy and prosperous future in Paris.

It was difficult for Nacha to say goodbye to my parents. Naturally, they worried about sending away their daughter so far away, at such a young age, just a short while after the couple had met. My father sent them off with a hefty dowry that included a wedding basket filled with comforters, tablecloths, and cutlery. My mother took off her necklace with four diamonds, along with a bracelet, both sentimental items given to her from my father, and handed them to Nacha to serve as precious reminders of their bond.

My sister settled in Paris. She wrote to us and sent us gifts for special occasions such as my bar mitzvah. I collected stamps from her letters. A few years earlier, my father had helped my

My sister with her husband, Moshe, in Paris, 1933.

Sruel before the war.

mother's sister, Becky, and her husband, Sam, to move to America, where they had settled in Greenville, Texas. There, they prospered in the clothing business. I looked forward to their letters—they would also send us American dollars—and I collected those stamps too.

My brother Sruel was 6 foot 2 and looked like a film star. He had gone to university in Warsaw to study business. Upon returning to Radom at age 22, he began working in a small clothing store. When my father saw that Sruel wasn't accomplishing his potential, he said, "Son, you don't need to work for anyone. I'm going to help you open up a store where you can do what you want." So my brother opened a store that produced high-end ladies' coats.

I looked up to Sruel. To me, he was everything the oldest brother should be—a strong man, the loyal guardian of our family, who watched over his parents and younger siblings. Whenever he saw me, he'd always hand me a few bucks for pocket change.

Most of the families I knew were less fortunate than us. In Poland at that time, as in many places in Europe, you were either up or down on your luck; there were wealthy landowners or poverty-stricken folk—the streets were filled with beggars—but hardly any middle class. Most of the Jews around us were manual workers—cobblers, carpenters, painters—and oh so poor. But no matter how poor, they always made sure to gather in the local *beit midrash*, the small house of study. On weekdays after school, I would stroll there with my father to pray the afternoon and evening services.

The hall was always full during prayer times. Simple pious folk stood in the corner, and when it came to the confessional passages, they would gently strike their hearts with their fists.

With tearful eyes and trembling lips, they would plead with G-d for forgiveness. I watched in amazement: *You have no money, no food, shabby clothes. All you do is study all day…What could you possibly have done wrong in your life?* I wondered.

The Richtmans, our neighbors, came from a family that owned a company that manufactured kitchen utensils. One brother had gone into the family business, prospered, and was living well, while the other brother resided in absolute ruin. He and his wife had five children, and they stayed in a broken-down shed. Amid the daily hardships and grind to subsist, their children led independent lives:

On Thursdays, crowds gathered in the marketplace as the farmers brought their produce, and the merchants brought materials to vend. Each of the Richtman children possessed a certain skill and would go to market to sell different items. At the end of the day, each returned home, bought a snack along the way, and ate alone. So while individuals earned pocket money, the family unit still never managed to make ends meet. They could barely afford food for meals, and they wore tattered garments.

My father didn't want to see them live that way. One day he stopped in to speak with Mr. Richtman, saying, "Listen, if everyone works together, you all can do much better. I'm going to come up with a plan of how to collaborate for the sake of all —and if my plan doesn't work, I'll help you out."

When my father saw that his counsel was to no avail, he stopped trying to advise Mr. Richtman. He gave him his space, and from then on, he just brought food over to their house. That was my first lesson of how the ability to earn does not necessarily equate to practical acumen of managing the finances.

CHAPTER 2
Life Lessons

When I was 6, I began school—cheder. The walk from our house to our school was half an hour each way. Radom was an industrial town of 80,000 inhabitants. Many Jewish prospered. Samuel Adler owned a large leather factory in town. Elias Tenenbaum, one of Radom's well-known industrialists, established a nail factory that supplied a great portion of Poland. The air in the streets was saturated with smells from the numerous factories, and smoke filled the city skies. Wagon drivers loaded with traveling merchants would congregate in the center of town.

The path to school was more serene, leading through fields of wheat stalks and red poppy flowers. The winters were bitter, snow white, and windy. I walked to school with my older brother Dovid. Sometimes along the way, we'd see a rock flying in our direction. Looking around, we'd notice some Polish schoolboys. "Hey, Jew—go back to Palestine," they'd shout.

We'd then take a closer look to check if they were around our size, and if so, we'd motion for them to walk over to our side of the street. We scuffled, and after we knocked the daylights out of them, we earned their respect and became friendly.

There were 10 children in my class, including my next-door neighbor Moshe Rappaport, Shimon Eisenman, Baruch Miller, and a few other friends. The teacher carried a wooden yardstick with which to smack the knuckles of any student who didn't pay attention. Sometimes he'd pull you by the ear.

At noon classes were dismissed for lunch. We'd run home, and my brother and I usually brought along one or two classmates. It was unthinkable to us to return to a house where we could enjoy a tasty lunch while the kid in the next seat couldn't find a meal at his house. Before we even stepped in the door, my parents, anticipating our hunger, would already have sandwiches prepared for everyone. Then we'd walk back together to finish the school day.

Before the war, television was scarce, and without the distractions of television or even radios in most homes, all our attention went to studying and reading. After school, I played soccer with Moshe Rappaport and other neighbors. We went inside for tea and cakes. My older siblings were fans of touring Yiddish theater groups; they attended plays and listened to Jewish musicians in our house on a gramophone. Occasionally my friends and I went into town to the cinema, which had begun to include sound. Films would begin with the famous lion roaring on the screen, and we would all jump back in our seats.

When I was 13, the Jewish cheder changed to an interfaith school consisting of Jews and Catholics. This change was prompted by some intermarriages in which those parents wanted their children to be exposed to both cultures—to also learn Yiddish and Hebrew. At that time in my life, I thought everyone in the world was either Jewish or Catholic. The school was jointly run by a rabbi and a priest. But as part of the agreement, the priest never mentioned religion—he concentrated only on teaching the Polish language.

The end of the week brought the Shabbos, which refreshed me. On Friday afternoon, we changed into our festive garb. My father returned early from work to help prepare for the royal day of rest. His brothers, who had settled in Sosnowiec, a mine region near the Czechoslovakian frontier, would sometimes visit our house with our cousins for the weekend. The warm aromas of my mother's dishes provoked anticipation for the night meal. Every room in our house was sparkling clean; calmness filled the air, and good wishes were on everyone's tongue.

The period immediately preceding sunset was filled with precious moments. My mother stood at the dinner table preparing her silver candelabra, custom-made with seven curving branches. She struck a match and delicately kindled the seven wicks, one flame representing the living soul of each member of our family. She then covered her eyes and stood motionless for minutes, in deep concentration as she whispered the Sabbath blessing, along with her most private prayers. As she lifted her hands and sunset advanced, we all approached each other with greetings of "*gut Shabbos.*"

Shortly afterward, my father would walk with my brothers and me to the grand synagogue on Podwalna Street, a large two-story brick building with high ceilings. All weekday activity had come to a halt. The streets had turned quiet, as nobody drove or lit a fire. From those quiet gloomy roads, we entered a world of majestic holiness, elegant chandeliers hanging over a cheerful room of radiant worshippers, all dressed in their finest clothes.

After the service, my father would always bring home guests from shul, including the rabbi, the *chazzan* (who led the congregation in prayer), and the *gabbai* (who assisted in the running of services). By that time, our dining room had been transformed into a palace. The Bobbe Raizel looked like a queen in her long flowing dress and a special *sheitel* she wore for the Sabbath. The lighting in the dining room was dim, and the white tablecloth glowed from the array of flickering flames atop the tall silver candleholders. Each place at the table was set with polished cutlery. The combination of fragrances from traditional Jewish foods—freshly baked challah loaves to searing hot chicken soup—was a heavenly delight.

My father stood at the head of the table and lifted his silver wine goblet to make *kiddish*, thereby sanctifying the Sabbath night, and we proceeded to the kitchen to wash our hands with a traditional rinsing cup before returning to eat bread. The meal began with a plate of carp and gefilte fish, followed by my mother's glistening golden chicken soup, chopped liver, and the main course of meat, and finally a rich compote made from pears and apples for dessert. My mother and grandmother always carried the plates to the table to serve the visitors, while my father focused on engaging the people. I noticed, however, that my father never touched his food until she sat down to eat hers. The guests would stay long into the night, singing festive *zemiros*, melodies.

During the day, when cooking was prohibited, two non-Jews, a man and his wife, were hired to prepare the hot meal. As we sat around the table to eat lunch, they would carry in two large pots of stew, and the most pleasing smell would again waft through the house. After lunch, we'd take family strolls in scenic parks.

That 24-hour period brought joy to everyone. My father loved hosting, and visitors always felt welcome in our house. The pride in seeing a vibrant household was visible on his face. Indeed, it was within the walls of his home that my father most enjoyed life.

As the Shabbos came to a close and the flames of the braided candle intertwined, goodness again was on everyone's mind; we wished each other "a *gut voch*"—a good week.

⟫•0•⟪

My father never preached kindness—he simply showed us care and gentleness and shared his time with us. He took great care in the way he handled the children—not only us, but our friends. They were in our house after school. They were our guests for Shabbat and festive meals.

"Every new day that G-d gives you," my father would often remark, "can always be a good one. But whether it *actually* turns out to be good will largely depend on your mindset." Whenever the snow and bitter cold prevented us from walking to school, it was never a day off—my father saw an opportunity to teach me and my brothers something about his business.

Even now, whenever the weather turns bad, I can hear his voice saying, "Well, it's too cold to go out—come over to the table." We would walk to the table and sit down next to him. He'd bring in some earrings, a necklace, a ring, or other merchandise that people had pawned. He'd lay the items on the table. "This is a sapphire, this is a ruby, and here's a nice diamond." He'd pick up a diamond and place it gently in my hand. "You see, a grade of 'D' is a bad grade in school, but a D flawless stone costs three or four times what you pay for a regular stone."

Or he'd say, "You see these—they're both gold, right? But this is 14-karat gold—it's very durable and has 58 percent pure gold. This is 18k gold, strong but quite not as durable. This will be a richer yellow." He'd also explain what each item could be used for and how to polish it carefully until it shone bright, always helpful to make a sale.

The practical details of gold, diamonds, and other precious items were not particularly fascinating for a young boy, but my father had a way of making anything interesting. We eagerly absorbed his words. We knew that if our father took the time to teach us something, it would later be valuable in life.

Indeed, we learned something from all he said — and more from what he never said. Never a harsh word came from his mouth, not to his family or when speaking about his fellow man. Growing up without ever hearing your father utter criticism, always encouraging us, it was easy to absorb his teachings.

CHAPTER 3
Liquor Bottles

We were born into a climate thick with persecution, where insults and danger were a regular component of life in Poland. The Poles had a common saying to the Jews, "Your buildings are yours, but the streets are ours."

In 1917, my family had barely escaped death from a widespread pogrom. According to my sister's account, as they hid in the nearby apartment of a friendly neighbor, they could hear the Bolsheviks banging on their front door with clubs and bayonets in hand. There was plenty of damage and victims in the neighborhood.

At the end of 1938, the Poles came out with a jingle about Maruszhko, an infamous bandit. "Hold up the Jews and take their money" was the popular verse. That was the first time I learned about a pogrom.

On Thursdays in Poland, farmers came to sell their produce at market. There were farmers, shoemakers, tailors, hat makers. In the small towns near Radom, before the war nobody had a car. One Thursday, Maruszhko waited until evening when the Jews returned home to unload their wagons. He and his cohorts ambushed them and robbed the peddlers while other groups of Poles went into the houses, struck down and murdered other Jews. During this pogrom, in the midst of the terror and tumult, a Jewish teen stood by his horse and buggy. He disconnected a wooden shaft from the wagon, hit the leader of the bandits in the head and killed him.

The police dragged him to the jailhouse in Radom. The next day, the newspaper headlines read, in Polish rhyme, "Jewish blood and Polish blood doesn't mix." When my father learned of the incident, he used to visit the young man in jail to bring him food every Friday. But after the Germans came in, they went through all the documents to find the Jewish prisoners, and quickly disposed of them.

⟫•◦•⟪

One customer came to my father to borrow money to open a restaurant. His storefront was located in a prime spot, in front of a meeting place for paid wagon drivers—similar to a central bus station of the day. The regular traffic allowed the restaurant to operate late at night. The restaurant was doing well, until the meeting place moved and the man went broke. Consequently, my father had to take it over.

Now, my father had never been in the restaurant business and had to learn quickly. One day he returned from the auction sales, where he acquired all types of goods at a lower price. That day he had brought home more than 100 empty wine and liquor bottles.

"Aren't they beautiful?" my father asked.

"They're just empty bottles," my mother said. "What on earth are we going to do with empty bottles?" But my father had an idea.

He filled the bottles, corked them, put a wax seal around the cork, and took them to his new restaurant, where he displayed them on shelves behind the counter. Now, anyone who walked in and saw a room full of bottles immediately realized they were not only in a restaurant but a bar. There was plenty of liquor, anything you wanted to drink. The fact that my father didn't have a liquor license — it was a dry area — was of no concern. Many Polish police officers were bribed by store owners. If a store owner wanted to stay open later than the law allowed, for example, all he had to do was pay.

In no time, the customers came streaming in. My father hired a manager to run the place. They served a variety of foods and desserts — all kosher — such as borscht, kreplach, *klops* (meatballs), raisin kugel, latkes, *lekach* (honey cakes), and more. These traditionally Jewish dishes were popular even with the Polish crowds. The place was lively. People met there to play cards while having afternoon tea and cake. And if one walked into this restaurant any given morning, 15 policemen could be seen sitting and eating breakfast — and none of them paid a dime for the meal. All the while, liquor was served from behind the counter.

Everything went well until some competitors got wind of my father's success — *shortly after the previous owner goes broke, the same restaurant is packed with people?* — and there must have been complaints. One day a group of men from the liquor control board stormed into the restaurant.

"What's going on?" the manager asked.

The head officer held up his badge. "We want all those bottles," he said, pointing to the display behind the counter.

"Okay, but please don't bother the customers," begged the manager. "Just let them finish eating."

The men began collecting the bottles from the shelves. Then they came to our house to arrest my father. Naturally, we were all shaken by the commotion. But my father did not seem fazed. "Everything's all right," he assured us. He stepped outside, talked to the officials, many of whom he apparently knew, and then came back inside as if nothing had happened.

But then came a court date. We were all tense and concerned that my father could be put in jail. *How long would he stay there? How would we get along without him around?* My mother and my brother Sruel accompanied him to the court. Six hours later, they returned. As soon as they walked through the door and I saw the expression on my mother's face, I could already tell how it had all turned out. She immediately recounted the details of the court case to me—a story she was fond of recalling from time to time.

When the hearing began, the judge asked: "Mr. Rzepkowicz, you don't have an advocate to represent you?"

"I didn't steal anything, Your Honor, so I don't need a lawyer," my father answered. So the hearing began. The prosecution presented all the evidence against my father.

"Are those your bottles?" they asked.

"Yes they are," my father answered. "Your Honor, do I look like a person who would steal anything?"

"You are not here about stealing," the judge tried to explain. "You're being charged with selling liquor without a license."

My father kept silent, but when it came time for the verdict, the judge said, "Mr. Rzepkowicz, get up. We're going to sentence you."

"Will you at least give me a chance to speak?" my father asked.

"Go ahead," said the judge.

"I loaned a guy some money to open a restaurant, and he couldn't pay me back. So I took over the business. I had never been in the restaurant business before this, and I just wanted to decorate the store—so I chose those nice bottles. Can an owner not decorate his store the way he pleases?"

Everyone in the courtroom began to snicker.

My father proceeded with his defense: "Judge, I told you. I didn't steal, and I'm not afraid. I just want to ask you—before you charge me with selling liquor, would you please open up those bottles and taste what's inside."

The judge smirked, shook his head, and motioned for one of the bottles to be brought to him. The security guard brought over the bottle and opened it before the judge. The judge poured a few drops on his hand and then tapped his wet fingers on his tongue. Suddenly, his expression changed to confusion. Smacking his lips together, he shouted, "This is water!"

One by one each bottle was brought up, tasted, and all were found to contain water.

"I told you," my father said, "I only decorated my store with *empty* bottles. They're not for sale!"

Fortunately, the officers hadn't bothered to check behind the counter. The case was dismissed.

But my father was not satisfied. Before leaving the courtroom, he had the chutzpah to make one last request. He asked the judge to please order those men to return all the bottles to the shelves in his store. "You took them all down," he said. "So you put them back up."

CHAPTER 4

"Choose Someone Else"

During a looming crisis, the approach of many parents these days is to shield their kids from the harsh reality. Better to wait until they mature, they figure, before revealing the extent of the danger and strife in the world. But growing up in Europe before the war, most parents I knew chose not to conceal the imminent danger from their children. Rather, they had open discussions with them. In our house, at least, we had plenty of those discussions. We heard that there would be a war soon—we just couldn't imagine what the war would bring.

German refugees in Poland brought bits of news of what lay ahead. From them we learned that the Germans had confiscated stores belonging to Jews, taken away their belongings, and created Jewish ghettos. We hadn't yet heard about murders. We were well settled in Poland. We had a close-knit family, plenty of friends. My father had a comfortable business, owned a nice house—nobody wanted to pick up and leave all that. And anyway, there was too little time to prepare.

In August 1939, I had just turned 16 years old when German soldiers stormed into Radom with huge heavy trucks. They burned our synagogue to the ground. They went around to the Jewish stores and told the owners to load all their merchandise into the truck. They then handed each owner a receipt from the Gestapo and told him where to go. The store owner naïvely thought that he was coming there to get paid for his merchandise. Instead, when he showed up to collect, he was beaten up, his receipt torn up, and he was sent home.

"I talked to the higher authorities in the Polish government," my father told us. "The war will be over in three months."

One day, the Germans showed up at my school. The officers escorted the rabbi (who was the co-principal with the priest), all the teachers, and students, without distinction, to a work site consisting of two piles of mud and stone.

In the years that would follow, I would become well acquainted with the trait of sadism. This was my first lesson. The principals and teachers were brought to the front to be used as examples—to demonstrate the labor to us. One man was given a bucket, the other a shovel. "Fill up the bucket, take it to the next pile, until there's nothing left in this pile," said the German commander. The faculty members did as instructed while the students watched. The German officers then made them repeat the process. "Bring it back to the other side."

Next it was our turn to suffer this worthless task. The officers beat young students for not working fast enough, sprayed us with a hose, and when someone tried to run and slipped, he got beaten more. After about six hours of work, we were weary and famished.

A group of students, drained from the labor, approached the principal, crying and begging for water to drink. The principal walked over to the German commandant and nervously asked if the schoolchildren could possibly get water to drink. The commandant told him to select one of the students to bring a bucket to the rest. For better or worse, I always pretended to be tough, not fearful. So when the principal asked for a volunteer, I immediately put up my hand.

I thought I was being selected to carry the water, but instead the commandant tied my hands. Two soldiers hung me from the branch of a tree. They then walked over with their German shepherd dogs, stood on either side of me, and struck my back with leather straps until my skin opened and blood began to stream. I suppose that was a message to the entire group—their way to instill fear. I was cut down and immediately forced back to work.

We continued working for another few hours, and again people came to the principals to complain. This time, the rabbi approached another student, and suggested that he go ask the commandant for some water on behalf of the group; naturally the child refused, fearing the same punishment for speaking up. The rabbi then came back to me. "Itzhele," as he called me, "we're all so thirsty. You're brave. Do you want to try again? Surely, they'll understand that it's urgent."

"I already took my beating," I told him. "I don't want a second portion—find someone else." The rabbi and the priest asked around but couldn't find another volunteer. Then the priest came over to plead with me.

I didn't want to refuse again. Instead, I told him, "Give me a few minutes by myself—I'll have to ask the Lord."

"What do you mean?" He looked shocked. "Have you ever spoken with G-d before?"

"No," I answered, "but there's always a first time."

I walked a few feet away from him, and with parched lips, mumbled my own prayer: "G-d, I am thankful to be a member of your chosen people, but this time, dear G-d, please choose someone else."

After a few minutes, the priest came back to me.

"So?"

"This time, G-d told me no!" I answered.

When the day was over, we were ready to collapse from exhaustion. They kicked us around some more, pushed people into the mud, and chased everyone home.

⟶•◦•⟵

When I arrived home, my parents took one look at my muddy, bloodstained clothes and sensed something dreadful had happened. But they hid their pain. Without uttering a word, my mother brought in a washing tub. She and my father cleaned me and treated my wounds. They fed me. Then we sat down at a table for one of those discussions.

"What kind of work did the Germans have you do?" my father asked.

I told him.

He immediately stood up and walked over to his small library of Jewish books. He returned with a Passover Haggadah, and began to flip the pages. I watched in confusion.

The sight and smell of the colorful, timeworn pages stirred up recollections of the Passover night; my mind began to flash with memories. Each year, during the days leading to the festival, we purged the entire house of any leavened products, just as Jewish law prescribed. My brothers and I would carry all the furniture outside into the courtyard so that my mother could clean. When the housework was complete, not a crumb or speck of dirt remained anywhere. The shelves were spotless. Even the bare floors shone. We exchanged all our usual utensils and dishware with another set, fit for Passover. Two days before the holiday, Mendel the baker sent over a stack of boxes with carefully wrapped *matzahs* inside.

Passover night, our dining room table was filled with family and guests. Even children would stay awake past midnight, reciting every word of the Haggadah—various passages relating the emancipation from Egypt. We eventually reached the meal, which opened with my mother's piping hot matzah ball soup, with its floating carrots and hefty *kneidlach,* so mouthwatering and healthful.

Pondering these memories, I looked back up at my father, waiting for him to speak. *What does that book have to do with what happened today?* I thought.

My father began reading: "We were slaves to Pharaoh in Egypt ..." then skipped to a passage, which he carefully read aloud in Hebrew—"and the Egyptians made their lives bitter with hard labor, with clay and with bricks and ... *with oppressive labor.*"

He stopped and looked up at me. "In the Holy Tongue, this expression for 'oppressive labor' is not just any type of hard work; it means toiling without accomplishing anything from your effort—useless work. That was Pharaoh's main goal, to break the Jewish spirit.

"My dear son," he continued. "The kind of work the Germans made you do today was of no use—except to try to take away your dignity, your childhood, and your intelligence."

The next day we returned to school, and our lives appeared to continue as normal. A month later, however, German soldiers were back.

CHAPTER 5

"Should Anyone Survive, Remember This Place"

March 1941, the Radom ghetto was established by the Nazis. A month later it was closed off from the outside. The ghetto was built for only 10,000 people —and there was enough food for only that amount—but it ended up holding a population of around 30,000. The German occupiers proceeded to collect all the Jews from the small townships and villages nearby and brought them in.

The main synagogues in the city were burned to the ground. Then came the rules—bulletins every hour on the hour —from the head of the occupied Polish territories. "By orders of *Gauleiter* Frank, any Jew walking on the sidewalk who sees a German soldier must immediately cross the street, and tip his hat." The noncompliance penalty was death. "Anyone caught with a radio will be killed."

A day later, another sign was up on the wall from the governor in Kraków. "Jews who own a radio must deliver the radio within 12 hours." Bulletins continued to come out. Then the Germans came up with rations—only so much bread distributed a day. Any Jew caught buying more food, or stealing, earned the death penalty. How much death can a person take?

To implement these punishments, there was, of course, no legal process: Every German soldier was now the judge, juror, and executioner. And they had plenty of fun. Sometimes they wouldn't kill you immediately—they'd first cut out your tongue or cut an ear off, before firing the pistol.

People's lives were turned upside down, and their priorities quickly changed to survival. The most pressing concern for parents in the ghetto became how to feed their children. I saw many a mother taking from her rations to feed her kids. It was the most natural maternal move to hand over a meager portion to a starving babe; however, giving away that piece of bread would often leave her without enough to survive.

From among the Jews, the Germans appointed a president of the ghetto, whose job it became to keep files on all the community members and perform other administrative tasks. Sometimes, he had to raise and deliver a certain amount of money by a certain date. Other times, he had to select young men for work.

The president of the Radom ghetto was a friend of my father, which came with some small privileges. He gave our family an exclusive apartment, situated away from the other houses, closer to the outside Aryan quarter.

Compared to our previous home, our new living quarters were skimpy, consisting of one room, two beds, and a little potbellied stove to cook and heat the house. A family of six, occupying a single room: My father, my brother Dovid, and I slept in one bed. Yankele slept with my mother in the other bed. My brother Sruel slept on the floor. It's the only way we could fit.

Our housing complex had a two-way entrance. One side faced the Aryan side, separated only by an iron fence. Thank G-d, we were three resourceful brothers. We got to know some handy fellows who could make keys. Two or three times a week

I used to remove my armband, marked with the yellow Star of David, and sneak into the Aryan district. I brought some gold rings, diamonds, or other small valuables and traded them for food—potatoes, flour, sugar, or whatever I could get hold of—and smuggled it back in. Every time I stepped out of our house, my father stood anxiously by the door, waiting for me to return, unsure if he'd ever see me again. I always came back.

The Gudstadt family was assigned to live in the quarters next door. Before the war, Mr. Gudstadt had operated a jewelry company and made a fortune. A small courtyard divided our residences in the ghetto. During one week, in the middle of the night, my father and Mr. Gudstadt went outside to bury the most prized belongings. They took me and my brother Dovid—the Gudstadts had no older children—to keep watch. "Should anyone survive, remember this place," they warned—"this will make you rich."

During such moments, apprehension heightens your senses. With one eye on the shovel and the other scanning the surroundings, I memorized every detail of that area.

⟫•◦•⟪

When the war was over, I traveled back to Poland with my wife. We visited the site of the one-room quarters in the ghetto, where a house now stood. The old structure had been torn down, and a renovated apartment stood in that place. A young Polish couple answered the door. "I used to sleep here with my family when it was a Jewish ghetto," I told them. "Do you mind if I look around?"

Reluctantly, they let me in. I walked through the rooms, trying to trace and envision the room where we once subsisted. Everything looked different. These walls, the ceilings, were all newly painted and modern. "I would be glad to pay you a few thousand dollars," I offered them, "if you would let my wife and me stay in this apartment alone tonight—just for sentiment's sake, to recollect the last days I spent here with my parents and siblings."

Had they agreed, I would have surely located the burial site. But I never had the opportunity to try. "Jew," the woman snapped, "if you don't get the hell out of our house, we'll have you killed." So we left. To this day, I have never returned.

⇒►◦◄⇐

Life in the ghetto was turmoil and terror. Every morning, the president of the ghetto was required to deliver a certain number of people for slave labor. The captain of the Jewish committee would say, "Tomorrow at 6 a.m., I need 500 men between the ages of 15 and 30." The police would come in the night, take you out of bed, and deliver you the next morning to the Germans.

The Germans rounded up Jews and made them load trucks with coal or wood. These sadists placed people in the exceedingly difficult work, such as being harnessed to a massive wagon filled with construction materials, and along with five other men, having to pull it to different locations, sometimes miles away. It was a task meant for horses. When the men finished a hard day of labor, they were sent back to the ghetto with a good beating.

Other times, they would give people a small tool, the size of a toothbrush, to sweep the streets. When, after two minutes of swiping dirt, the bristles began to disappear, the German guard then instructed the sweepers to use their fingers. They watched as skin peeled off, blood trickled from hands, and made them continue cleaning.

View of the main square of the ghetto in Radom.
(Courtesy of United States Holocaust Memorial Museum.)

Polish farmers sell their produce in Radom market.
(Courtesy of United States Holocaust Memorial Museum.)

At night, German soldiers could come unannounced into the homes. If a German soldier walked in and beat up a father, the children had to stand by and watch. Can you imagine what that does to a child? The fear was terrible. Every hour that passed without a knock on the door, guards shouting — *"raus, raus"* (get out) — was a relief. That's how we lived, day in and day out.

One night, we heard footsteps near the door of our house, then a loud knock on the door. My little brother, Yankele, screamed, "They're coming for us — Sruelik, hide! Dovid, hide! Itzik, hide!" Of course, in a one-room house there was nowhere to hide.

But this time, we received an unexpected visit from our previous non-Jewish neighbor, who had managed to track down our family's whereabouts. He had worked as the district attorney in Radom. His daughter had attended the same university as Sruel.

My father let him inside. He approached my father with a proposition: "Lazer, we've been neighbors for a long, long time," he began. "We both see what's happening to the Jews. Your son Sruel and my daughter Mary went to school together. Now, we both know that these two kids fell in love, and that they've been hiding their relationship. Sruel is a fine young man, and with my connections in the government, it won't be difficult for me to arrange false papers for him. With your permission, let Sruel and Mary get married and move to Warsaw."

The idea of intermarriage would have previously been inconceivable for my father, which is why Sruel had never mentioned the relationship to our family. But in such dire circumstances — to save the life of his son — my father had to consider such a proposition.

"If you agree," the neighbor continued, "Sruel and Mary can bring along your youngest son, Yankel, to pose as their child."

My father agreed. Sruel and Mary went to live in Warsaw, along with my little brother, Yankele, who was 5 years old at that time. Sruel promised to sneak into the ghetto to visit us whenever he could.

CHAPTER 6

Mother's Milk

I n August 1942, the Germans began "cleansing" the ghettos, periodically removing large groups of Jews and deporting them on trains to various extermination camps. We never knew when our time would come. The anguish began to eat away at my father; his health deteriorated. He became weaker until he was confined to bed. I was lying in bed next to him, holding him, when he passed away.

The authorities would never allow Jews to hold a funeral and provide a proper burial. But my brother Dovid and I managed to smuggle his body outside the ghetto with a horse and buggy, which we loaded with big boxes of trash. We sped to a nearby Jewish cemetery. There, in an empty spot of earth, we frantically dug a ditch and buried our father. With little time to spare, the best marker we could manage was to rip off a large piece of cardboard on which we wrote his Hebrew name and date of passing with a stick of charcoal.

Now my father, my hero, was gone from my life; I was just 18 years old. At that moment, I resolved to take him with me—all the wisdom and values he had imparted to us while in this world—wherever I would go. So I did—and he never steered me wrong.

⇒▶•◀⇐

In early autumn I was walking home, dressed in slacks and a wool sport coat, still wearing a band around my arm with a yellow Star of David. As I neared the ghetto, I noticed German officers rounding up Jews. Instinctively, I sensed trouble. I quickly ripped off my armband and dashed to find a place to hide. I crossed the street behind the prison and headed for a church near our former house.

On my way, I noticed a young Jewish mother nursing her baby. She was sobbing. The tears continued to flow as she changed her infant's cloth diaper, wrapping a new cloth twice around the child's bottom, then bundled the baby in a heavy blanket. *Why is she crying like that?* I wondered. I peered around the corner, waiting to see how this scene would unfold.

The mother gently kissed the infant's head, held it close to her neck for a few seconds, and then slowly placed the bundled child at the entrance to a nearby apartment stairwell. She knelt down, leaned her face against her child's once more, before running away to await her own dismal fate from the German officers around the corner.

(Throughout my years, in my darkest moments of doubt, that mother's pain has remained at the forefront of my mind.)

I stood frozen, stunned by what I'd just seen. In such critical seconds, I still couldn't keep my mind from drifting, imagining what might become of this child. *Maybe, if everything went as that mother hoped, a righteous gentile would find her baby, bring it into the house, baptize the baby, and raise it as a Christian. And then there might come a time, perhaps on the deathbed of some adoptive parent or grandparent, when the news would be broken: "Many years ago, the Germans were sending off Jews in our area to their death. Someone left you on our doorstep—you almost certainly come from Jewish parents."*

I snapped back to reality; soldiers were coming. I had to move. I dashed inside the church, flung open the door of the sanctuary, then ran through the aisles and crouched behind a statue of the Virgin Mary so nobody could see me. An older nun was the only person in the building at the time—but she didn't appear to notice my entering. Just then, I heard the dreaded sound of boots and German voices in the hall. A few seconds later, two SS soldiers came storming in with their German shepherds, leather whips, and guns.

"Are there any Jews around here?" they asked the nun.

"No, I'm here alone," she replied.

G-d works in mysterious ways, and amazingly, the soldiers searched the premises and then left without letting their dogs sniff around. (To this day, I believe they were miraculously blinded.)

As I stood up from behind the statue, the sister of the church noticed me and gasped in shock, jumping back. She immediately ran to the statue and started praying in Polish—"Mother Mary, forgive me, for I lied," she pleaded. "I said that I was alone but now I see that I lied…"

I walked up to her. "You didn't lie," I told her, "you didn't see me."

"What I said wasn't true," she answered matter-of-factly.

"Well, did you know I was hiding here?" I asked.

"Of course not," she snapped, "otherwise I would have told them the truth—that you were there." She then began to hurry toward the door to go after the soldiers.

"Well," I retorted, "you run after them, and I'll tell them *you* hid me—then they'll take you along with me." She stopped.

I headed for our home in the ghetto. When I arrived, I found an empty house. I ran to my Bobbe Raizel's apartment. It was also empty. I never saw my family again.

"If you have years to live, you'll survive anything."

— Yiddish adage

CHAPTER 7

I Would Take Out the Trash

"*A rbeit macht frei*—work sets you free." That was the slogan at the gate of the slave labor camps that the Germans had prepared.

To make it there, we—the remnants of the Radam ghetto—first went through a selection: *"Vi alt bistu?"* (How old are you?)

"*Recht* [to the right]," the guard motioned to one Jew, "*links* [left]" to another, "*links, recht…*"

As the crowd was separated into two areas, I noticed the older, stronger people stationed to the right side while the frailer and younger people were being sent left. So when it came my turn, I lied about my age. I was tall and athletic and so was sent right. That's how I was sent to a labor camp instead of to the gas chambers.

Shortly after I entered the labor camp my name was no longer Itzik—I was now a number, 828, the identity I would carry for the next few years. "From now on, your livelihood will consist of two slices of bread at night," we were told. The bread was black and stale, and the slices were skinny. "In the morning, we'll give each of you two cups of coffee." It was ersatz coffee, with saccharin.

Then the guard showed us what we were going to receive for lunch. "If you work hard, you're going to get some soup." If the cup of water they gave us was dirty enough, it resembled soup, but we could hardly ever find a trace of a turnip or potato peel inside. Sometimes, just as a craving prisoner lifted his cup against his mouth to devour his morsel of nourishment, one of the sadistic guards would walk by and slap the cup away, the cup flying forward and the soup spilling on the ground.

I remember hearing prisoners sing solemn ditties, with phrases like "If you lose your piece of bread, you won't see tomorrow." We didn't know about crematoriums yet. But the songs themselves foreshadowed our fate.

Some people could not cope with these circumstances. I watched civilized humans changing into wild beasts, educated men from well-to-do families, former members of high society, snatching food from their neighbor, even stealing from people in their own family. And in such a case, when one steals, it's not simply stealing a piece of bread—you take away their soul.

The sadists figured out how long the average person could work on that type of diet. If you worked for a month, six weeks, maybe two months—eventually you'd end up by the fence. The fence is where people could lie down to rest for a while. But once you lay down, you couldn't get that cup of water anymore, nor anything to eat. And if you don't get anything to eat, you cannot walk. And if you can't walk, you can't work. And if you can't work, well...They stacked up corpses by the fence like firewood.

Sometimes they'd pull random prisoners out of line and bring them to the fence. A few times I was chosen to accompany the guards. When I got to the pile of bodies, they sprayed them with naphtha, kerosene. Then one of the guards handed me a box of matches. "Burn them!" he said.

I took out a match, but before I could strike it, I heard a voice hollering from the pile— "Hey, hey!" I looked down and saw a teenage boy. "If I can get a sip of water, I can still work."

I turned around and told the commandant, "There's a young man down there who's still alive, says he can work if he can drink something."

"You throw that match now," barked the commandant, "or I'll throw it—except you'll be in the pile with them."

———✥———

In the labor camps, I continued my brave but sometimes foolish habit: Whatever job they asked for—whether I had experience or not—I would put up my hand to volunteer. Whether it was a tailor, a barber, a shoemaker, painter, carpenter, I figured I was a quick learner and could puzzle it out once I arrived at the job. Sometimes it worked; other times I was given a bloody beating.

One day they requested a tailor. Eight of us offered our services. We arrived and discover they needed people to make uniforms. We stood there looking at tables with needles and threads, scissors, and fabrics—and nobody knew how to measure or cut. When our inexperience was revealed, we took a beating.

"Anyone here a barber?" they asked one day. When I volunteered, they sent me into the guardhouse to cut the hair. *Now I'm really doomed,* I thought. But G-d helped me; sure enough, I managed to cut hair, and nobody complained. I even used a blade to shave the guards without my hand shaking. Then, when they sent in a young German who was an experienced barber to work alongside me, I figured I was in trouble. "You know, I'm not really this type of stylist," I commented to him. "I keep the cuts simple." The next day, I was moved to cut prisoners' hair with hand-held clippers.

Eventually, I was assigned to work in the ammunition factory assembling guns. The factory production went from raw materials to finished materials, and from those finished materials we'd put the gun together. There were two shifts, each lasting around six hours. After the first shift, we had to clean up the department to get everything ready for the second shift. I would take out the trash bags. Sometimes when I'd walk outside, I would see familiar faces — old Polish neighbors, teenagers with whom I had gone to school — now collaborators, proudly wearing swastikas. When I would greet them, they'd pretend they didn't know me.

At that stage, most of the officers in the camp were Polish police and Kapos, Jewish prisoners in privileged positions. These Jews were not treated like the rest of us — they received extra rations and other perks. They wore special navy blue armbands with KAPO in bold, bright letters. German commanders appointed them to supervise and keep a close eye on other inmates — and, if need be, to denounce them. Along with these duties, they were given authority to push us around. Many of the Kapos, invigorated with their newfound power, were cruel and ruthless.

The head of the Kapos was a Jewish man by the name of Heil Friedman. He didn't even have to put on prisoners' garb — he wore civilian clothes. He marched around with a leather whip. He'd kick you in your behind, smack you, and scream profanities: "Get moving, you son of bitch." The funny thing is that he came from a reputable family in Radom who had owned a leather business. But he was as mean as they came.

Soon Jews began arriving from other countries — from Austria, France, and Holland. They were more educated and sophisticated than the Jews from Poland. And they didn't expect what was coming next; they thought they were just relocating.

Because of their lifestyle, the aristocratic climate from where they originated, most of them did not have the resilience to handle the sudden change in conditions. So they faded quickly.

I remember watching a noble Jewish lady coming off the train. After the grit and pain we experienced on a daily basis, the colorful sight of these beautiful people arriving, well-to-do and stylishly dressed, immediately caught your attention. Her thick flaxen locks flowed over her white fur coat; she wore long leather gloves, diamonds, and sleek boots. As she stepped out into the fresh breeze, she pulled out lipstick from her pocket and applied it gently on her lips. She perused the surroundings, as if she were visiting a resort. A Kapo walked over to help her take down the suitcase, and she reached into her purse and pulled out a bill to tip him.

I observed the other Kapos watching her too. I noticed how they traded looks, laughed to each other, mocking her naïveté. A few hours later, she looked like a different person—her belongings seized and her hair shaven, she stood in line wearing a prisoner's smock and wooden clogs. A few days later, she was a corpse being stacked against the fence. That degeneration was commonplace for us, like living within an endless horror show: "Now you see me—now you don't."

——⟫•0•⟪——

I have always been a good reader of faces. Among the harsh steely visages and icy gazes of the cruel guards in the camp, there was a Polish officer who had a more pleasant countenance. He was around 6 foot 2 with blond hair and light green eyes and in his mid-20s. He displayed a tough exterior, yet his soft smile signaled a nice man beneath the surface. I must have been a little crazy at the time to take such initiative—it was dangerously risky to approach any officer—but I decided to toss him a compliment.

"You have the kindest smile," I told him one day. At first he just stared at me in silence. The next day, I repeated the compliment, and again the day after.

After the third time, he began speaking to me. Sometimes he'd walk over and hand me a pear, or an extra piece of bread. Over the next few weeks, we became better acquainted. He always seemed to have plenty of questions for me.

"Tell me, what type of work do you do?"

"I work in the ammunition factory," I answered. "I assemble guns."

"What gun?"

"The Vis."

"What parts?"

"Mainly the barrel—the part that sends the bullet to the target—but I've handled the firing pin and the frame too. Between shifts, I also bring out the trash."

Then one day he opened up. "I'm a partisan," he said. "I work with the Polish underground."

As time went on, he used to bring me news of what was happening in other camps. "Should you ever be asked to undress and told you are going to shower, you will see an entrance. But when you go in to take a shower," he warned, "the doors will close up on you. That means there won't be an exit."

One Friday, he approached me and asked, "Do you have any family on the outside?"

"I don't know what happened to my mother and middle brother," I answered. "But my oldest brother and baby brother are living in Warsaw under false papers. They go under the last name of Stasz."

"Well," he said, "I'm going to Warsaw for the weekend. I'll do my best to find them." When he walked away, a sudden dread came over me. *Oh, no, what have I done?*

——⟫•०•⟪——

That night, I couldn't sleep. I had been trying to please an elder guard, answering his questions. I figured that if you want something, you have to give up something, but you can also make a mistake in doing so. After all, I barely knew this man. My thoughts raced: *What if he wasn't from the Polish underground, if he was just using me to get information — and now I've told him everything he wanted to know. That would mean the end of me. And not only have I endangered my own life, but I've jeopardized the safety of my two brothers and Mary.* I waited with anguish to see him on Monday.

Monday morning, he eyed me from a distance. Eventually, when no other officer was around, he called me over. "Here, take it," he said, as he swiftly handed me a folded piece of paper. "Go now to the corner — as if you're going to the bathroom — read it and dispose of it immediately."

I opened the paper and saw a note in Yiddish. I knew that the handwriting had to be from my brother Sruel.

My dear brother Itzik,

I received a visit from the man you sent. I hope that you know this gentleman well, as you have entrusted our lives to him. We are still alive in Warsaw. Have faith. Be strong. And with G-d's help, you'll survive.

— Sruel

Sure enough, the man was from the underground. When I came to thank him, he said, "You entrusted yourself to me. Now I entrusted myself to you. But now I need something from you."

"What do you need from me?" I asked. "I'm not a free man—I can't do anything for you."

"Yes you can," he said. "From this moment on, you work for me. You are going to be a thief."

"What do you want me to steal?"

"Before you come to take out the trash, every day I want you to place a few parts in each bag, enough to make two or three guns. When you take out the bags, I'll be there to take them."

I followed his instructions, and every day when I stepped outside to throw the trash bags onto the truck, I'd hand them over to him. He'd load them into a truck and take them away.

So he made a thief out of me. In return for the favor, he'd bring me a few slices of bread, a potato, an apple, or a pear. This deal kept me alive for around a year, until 1943, when the Germans began rounding up more Jews to send away.

CHAPTER 8

He Never Used a Bullet

By the winter of 1943, we were down to a few thousand prisoners. We heard the Russian army was getting close. The Germans were clearly nervous. During a lineup, the SS men taunted us, "You Jews, you think you have it bad with us—but if the Russians come in, then you'll find out what real badness is." In truth, we would've been relieved to see anybody who didn't wear a Nazi uniform.

The Nazis sent us on a march—around 35 kilometers. From Radom, we walked to Kozienice. For days we didn't get a sip of water or anything to eat. If someone found a worm, they considered it a feast. Those who were too exhausted to walk were shot. Lots of people were dying. At nightfall, there were no accommodations to rest—wherever they decided to stop, that's where you slept. It was freezing, so sometimes you lay on dead bodies to keep warm.

From Kozienice we went to Kielce. We were then taken in boxcars to Kraków, and finally we arrived in Auschwitz, the infamous extermination camp.

⟞⟐⟜

Every prisoner, at one point, had to undergo the ultimate trial of pain. We had a common saying, "The end of the road is drawing near—but you only die once."

It seemed my time was coming soon after we arrived in Auschwitz. We were let out of the packed boxcars. Finally, some fresh air, but the guards never gave you much time to breathe. They always kept you moving.

The first sense one got from the camp was the eerie stench coming from tall smokestacks of the ovens where they burned the bodies of prisoners (more than 1,440 corpses every 24 hours). The Germans designed those crematorium chimneys tall, so the smell of scorching human flesh wouldn't be too intolerable. But for anyone who walked around the premises, once that deathly scent enters your nose, it remains in your brain for the rest of your time on Earth; I can still smell it.

"Undress!" a thunderous voice echoed. "Women on one side, men on the other." By that time, one could hardly tell the difference between a male and female; we were just walking bones.

As we began to undress, we knew something new was happening. Many prisoners carried a small photograph or something we treasured. When they took you away to the camp, a mother could take off her earring, maybe her little gold chain, a Star of David, a bracelet, or a tiny diamond, sew it into the clothes. "Take it with you. Maybe you'll be able to get a piece of bread for that." But if anyone was caught hiding an object, such as a family picture from home or a piece of food, they'd be punished.

Once everyone was undressed, we were told—"You're going to the shower!"

When I heard those words, I remembered what the officer from the Polish underground had said to me: "There may come a time when you will be asked to undress for a shower. But when you go in, the doors will close up on you. That means there won't be an exit."

At that moment, I decided to say one last personal prayer. I put my hands over my eyes and began: *"Shema Yisroel…"* (Hear, O Israel: G-d is our Lord, G-d is one.—Deuteronomy 6:4.)

We were marched into a chamber. I waited to die. The faucet was turned on—but there was no gas; only water came out.

⸻⬦⸻

We dressed and stepped onto a lot for a roll call. Some higher-ranked German officers came to look through the crowd and test our condition, like a rancher would go through his cattle. Then the "angel of death"—Josef Mengele, known for torturing prisoners in the guise of medical research—arrived on the scene. The notorious young doctor stood there, a slim man with perfectly combed hair and polished boots, slyly surveying us with his stony eyes while he smoked a cigarette with his gloved hand.

Unlike other officers, he didn't handle the selection directly with his hands. Instead, he held a stick with a sharp point. When he waved the stick to the right side, you went right, and then you got prodded with his stick. It stung into your side, so you moved left—then he jabbed you from the other side. The line to which he finally sent you decided your fate. With a cruel pleasure, he determined life or death. According to reports, he alone casually sent four hundred thousand souls—infants, children, mothers and fathers, elderly—to the gas chambers and ovens.

Hungry and dirty as we were, we used to pass by a sewer to wet our hands, wetting our tongue, or maybe there was a little vegetable peel. Nobody cared how muddy it was—you put it in your mouth just in case it could nourish you. On the way to the roll call, my childhood friend Moshe Rappaport had picked up something from the ground. An SS officer by the name of Jakob

60

Holz was in charge of the guard towers. He had been watching from his tower and immediately came down.

"What did you just put in your mouth?" he asked Moshe.

"I found a bean lying on the ground, so I swallowed it," Moshe answered fearfully.

Suddenly, I and another kid were called over, and the three of us were walked away from the group. The officer tied Moshe's hands. Then he pulled out his bayonet and gave it to the other kid.

"Open up his stomach." Shuddering, the kid inserted the blade into Moshe's stomach.

The officer turned to me. "Now you go in there and find it."

So I got on my hands and knees to dig through my best friend's insides—my neighbor, the boy I used to sit next to in class, play soccer with after school—only to discover a sliver of a diamond. I stood up and gave it to the German. We could not take Moshe back to the group for the roll call.

Walking back to the roll call line after such an ordeal, I figured I'd be exempt from any wrath—at least for a few minutes. But I was soon next in line. Mengele scrutinized me and discovered that I had a little gold filling in the back of my mouth —I was then almost 20 years old and didn't even remember having it done. I had no idea what was coming next. He grabbed another teenager out of the line and handed him a rusty pair of pliers. *What are they going to do with me?* I thought.

Mengele instructed the teen to pull all of my teeth. One by one, he fastened the pliers and yanked each of my teeth. A boy pulling out teeth takes time, and tons of effort. Along with the teeth, he mangled my gums. The blood streamed from my mouth and froze on my face as I returned to the line. With the roll call still in session, I couldn't even get a sip of water—so I rinsed my mouth with my own urine.

From that time on, I was left without a tooth in my mouth. But my time was not up yet. As the Yiddish adage goes, "If you have years to live, you'll survive anything."

After only a day in Auschwitz, we were sold to Wernher von Braun, the man building rockets to send to outer space.

⟫·◦·⟪

From Auschwitz, we were taken to Vaihingen an der Enz. Though we had heard that we would be working in a factory where they built missiles, we found no trace of a factory. Instead, we saw a camp and construction site fortified with double barbed wire, overseen by watchtowers, and cordoned off with SS troops. Inside were stone quarries.

This camp had been built as part of a secret program with the alias "Stoffel" to relocate Messerschmitt aircraft manufacturing plants underground, protected from Allied bombing raids. Even the farmers nearby needed a pass in order to work in their fields. The underground facilities were constructed in conjunction with the quarries in the area.

To prepare for an armament factory, we were assigned to start knocking out stones, transporting the rocks and rubble, sand, and gravel. We worked for six months, 12 hours a day, under dire conditions. It never seemed to end.

In the camp, there was an officer who walked with a limp. He had previously been a flier, until part of his foot was shot off. When he recovered, they appointed him as a commandant for us. Somewhere along the line, he must've graduated from the school of sadism.

He introduced himself to us by declaring with a shrewd smile, "I have never used a bullet in all my time here. And I don't plan to use any bullets on you."

We were initially relieved to hear that. In other camps, we'd watched Nazi guards shooting Jews for sport; they leisurely lined up people, who were worth less to them than stones on the ground, then took turns firing from a distance.

But, you see, the war was dragging, and this commandant had discovered creative ways to save bullets. We'd stand for a roll call. He'd pace back and forth in front of us, holding a plate. On the plate lay a nice slice of torte, a colorful pastry, or a five-layer cake. He'd pretend to place a small piece in his mouth, casually dropping the rest on the ground, and then walk away.

Suddenly, 50 starving skeletons morphed into a mass of roaring lions—charging toward one spot, hands flailing, clawing at each other for any remnants of that piece—trampling anything in their path. When the pile of bodies cleared, a dozen lay dead because they were too weak to stand.

His common pleasure was *retekh*—those big red radishes. He must have figured that if he can kill dozens of prisoners with just one tiny piece of cake, he could kill more with vegetables. So he'd walk behind the fence with a plate of frozen radishes, fling one over his shoulder, and watch as a crowd of people would scamper to snatch it; another pile of dead bodies.

In the end, he was honest: He never used a bullet—he didn't need bullets to kill.

———◦◦◦———

Those who survived continued to work, loading bombs. When we got through loading bombs, they sometimes took us out to do demolition work. When we heard sirens, we knew the Allied forces were close. The Germans knew it too. They were nervous, and as soon as they heard bombs, they ran down to a shelter.

But for us, the sound of falling bombs was the most beautiful music to our ears. Once the Germans ran for cover, we were told to walk outside and dismantle any bombs that didn't explode. I was a quick learner, and after a few trials, I could dismantle a bomb and put it back together.

But when I went out, I also saw houses being bombed. That spelled opportunity. Against their orders, I didn't go to look for bombs—nobody could see me anyway—instead I wandered into the houses. I walked straight in the kitchen, inspected the place for a left-over piece of bread or an old potato. While bombs were blasting through open air, I grabbed whatever food I found there. The only problem then was that I had no place to hide it. The wooden shoes they had given me had flimsy soles. Soon after, I lost the soles—I was left with shoe tops but no bottoms —so I tore off paper from cement sacks and tied them with wire around my feet.

With no option of hiding anything in my shoes, I filled my pants with food. Arriving back to the other prisoners, we used to have a party.

The bombing continued. Whatever Americans or the British or the Russians dropped, we were supposed to dig out of the ground. We played with those bombs as a kid kicks around a soccer ball. We tossed them back and forth to each other for fun. Nobody was afraid. And thank G-d, nobody died from explosives—but then again, one of those red radishes killed dozens of people. G-d works in mysterious ways.

CHAPTER 9
We Never Cried

Going from one camp to another, if you lived, it was only by the grace of G-d. Hessental was like any other camp, with one exception: In the other camps, we went through some type of disinfection where they sprayed us with chemicals to kill the lice. Not here; the lice were eating us alive.

Our previous commandant from the Vaihingen made occasional visits to Hessental and provided their guards with some more brutal ideas to save bullets. Sometimes when prisoners grew too sick or feeble for the labor, the guard would stand two men back to back, and suddenly thrust a big bayonet straight through the midsection of both, disposing of two in one shot.

In the wintertime, the SS guards used to wear heavy coats over their gray wool uniforms. They had gloves and mufflers, and fur boots on their feet. When it got dark, they made fires, drank whiskey, and roasted meat on a spit.

From a distance, we could hear their laughter and merry toasts; we saw them dining next to the warmth of flames. Our only belongings were a faded prison outfit and a little jacket, no underwear. We fought through malnutrition. We lay on the freezing ground. In the morning, half of the people were dead from frost.

All winter, I had gone around with paper wrapped around my feet. Sometimes you walked barefooted in ice. Our life didn't have a human being's quality in it. You were so filthy a dog wouldn't even bite you. We shivered at the hands of cold winds;

we craved a sip of water. At that point, I must have weighed around 80 pounds. You often ask yourself, *Oh, G-d, what will be next?*

Sometime around July of 1944, we left on a march to Dachau that seemed to last for weeks. The first several days, lots of people died. Sometimes you'd see a prisoner who, compared to the rest of us, looked like an athlete. They were the ones who used to work in the kitchen, with plenty to eat. But these guys were the first to fall. See, if your stomach was already shrunken, you didn't need the food. Because they were used to their daily nourishment in the kitchen, and here there was no food for several days, they rapidly collapsed.

Along the way, the Germans picked us up in the forest and took us in boxcars to Dachau. In the boxcars, they always crammed in too many people; our shriveled bodies bumped against each other, stacked like wet sardines in a container. As the train moved, you'd close your eyes and lean your head against someone's shoulder, open up your eyes and discover that you were resting against a dead man.

<hr/>

When we first arrived in Dachau, roll calls were six or seven times during a 24-hour period; day and night we were being counted. During that time, I met two men around my age. I recognized their faces from other camps, but this time we shared the wooden shelf where we slept. You see, we didn't have any beds; we had wooden shelves, which could house 12 people. They stuffed 25 people inside.

Most prisoners didn't talk much to one another, but the three of us became friends. Leibel was the son of a Hassidic rabbi from Poland. The other young man, Velvel, came from Austria, where his parents had owned a prosperous printing company. We made an agreement among ourselves: If anyone had advice about how to better survive, he would share it.

Now, the first thing that happened in the camps is your mind dried up, and then hope drained from your heart—you have nothing to look forward to. And when your mind goes, the sadness helps you die sooner. "Are we ever going to be able to see anyone from our family again?" people would say. And so when you lie down to go to sleep, you were certain you were going to die. You didn't know where or when it would be—but sooner or later, you felt you'd be gone.

The rabbi's son was a wise man. "The first rule," he said, "is that whenever one of us feels like breaking down, whether from the hunger, torture, or illness—thinking *How can I possibly withstand this much longer?*—we are never going to speak about those bad thoughts. Instead, at that moment, we will sing a little together."

And so, whenever we were around each other, we never cried. Our mouths were parched; we were starving; we didn't own anything in the world—but thank G-d, we still found a way to stay happy people. We never dwelt on pains and hardships. Instead, we'd reminisce about good memories from our families and upbringing. We helped one another with a good word— "Hey, this war will not last forever."

We even formed our own three-man band. Of course, we had no instruments, but we could still tap on our shoulder or our knee while we sang together, just to keep our spirits high. The rabbi's son had a talent for composing songs. He'd come up with beautiful lyrics, uplifting rhymes that can only be truly appreciated in Yiddish:

Don't ever say these are the last steps you'll take.
Don't ever lose hope, don't lose your faith.
The sun will shine for us one day.
We're going to be helped; we're going to be saved.

All lots have already been cast.
Be assured your time [to walk free] will come fast…"

That's how we spoke, and if you say it enough, it penetrates your mind. Having these companions also helped me keep my dignity. Other people just let themselves go, and eventually the lice ate them alive. When winter arrived, I used to get up in the middle of the night to walk outside into the snow, undress completely, and scrub myself clean.

To this day, when I feel sick and weak, and it's so soothing to stay in bed—I can't lie there for too long. *If you rest for too long, you'll get used to the bed, and you'll linger there,* I think to myself. But if I get up, drink a bit, and move around, I know I'll eventually feel better.

———⟫•◦•⟪———

One morning, a high-ranking officer showed up and asked if anyone was familiar with printing. The Austrian fellow, whose parents had owned printing businesses, naturally raised his hand. As usual, I also volunteered. The three of us were taken to a brick building—it was dark; nobody could tell from the exterior what was going on inside—and led into a brightly lit warehouse.

Turns out, when the Germans saw that bombing the British was not as successful as they'd hoped, they revived an operation to forge British banknotes. The original plan, Operation Bernhard, was to drop the notes over Britain to cripple the British economy. Now prisoners from various concentration camps were being selected for the program.

We worked in the storeroom down there for a few weeks. The Austrian fellow, who had expertise in printing techniques, assisted with the forgery. We knew nothing about printing; we just cleaned trays, spread the ink, let the papers dry and organized them.

———◆———

April 1945: Everyone awoke to the sounds of bombs raining down. The Allied forces were advancing. Guards led us into the nearby woods, on another dead march. For the next few days, we must have marched anywhere between 10 and 25 kilometers at a time. Along the way we heard rumors that we were soon going to be transported in boxcars to the Black Forest, where they planned to dynamite the trains and tear us all apart.

Then something must have happened—perhaps because German trains and trucks were under attack by American fighter planes at the borders of the camps—and we ended up back on the grounds in Dachau. The work schedule resumed, but the closer the US Army divisions got, the fewer the number of Nazi soldiers who remained in the camp. No more roll call. No more food.

As the typhus epidemic spread, I fell terribly ill. One of the guards directed me to the infirmary to recover. I was running a high fever; my mind was blank; I was gasping for breath. All I saw was darkness, and I was so dizzy I could hardly walk straight.

With all that, G-d still sent me a gust of common sense. As I stepped through the doorway of the infirmary, I realized that most of the people who entered through the front were being carried out through the back, dragged like a sack of potatoes toward the ovens, then tossed aside and piled up like logs in front of the crematoriums. I stood still for a moment—then I immediately moved backward and I walked out.

Over the next few days, I did my best to return to work. But by that time, I weighed close to 69 pounds and could no longer stand. Eventually, I collapsed from exhaustion. Soon I lay around the corner from where the crematoriums stood—I smelled death creeping near—and anticipated my turn. It happened, however, that the Nazis had run out of coal to burn bodies; corpses were stacking up quicker than they could be pulled away and buried.

I don't know how long I lay on that ground, waiting to pass on, but the next thing I remember is a loud voice calling out in Yiddish:

"Don't be afraid anymore. You are all free men! You are free."

I pried open my eyes and looked up. All I could make out was a blurry image of two shining silver bars on the shoulder of a soldier. To be sure, I couldn't tell the difference between one uniform and another, but the tenor of his voice and the Yiddish words let me know I had nothing to fear—I was certain it was a messenger sent from heaven. Indeed, above me stood a fine-looking Jewish captain of the American Army.

That day of liberation, April 29, 1945, I consider as my second birth. I lay in that spot laughing and weeping for what seemed like hours until the Jewish captain came back to me, bent down next to me, and said: "We're going to take you to a place to clean you up. They're going to feed and nourish you back to health." And that's exactly what happened.

*You have to take the good with the bad,
mix it up, and make it all good.*

CHAPTER 10
I Suddenly Encountered Angels

After the liberation, our clothes were burned, and we were cleaned up. But most survivors, those who managed to regain their health, still had nowhere to live. They could not leave Europe due to strict immigration policies in British Palestine, the United States, and elsewhere, which had quotas and restrictions. Thousands of Jews were gathered into camps that the Allies had established, referred to as DPs—displaced persons camps. Some were even stationed in the concentration camps behind barbed wire fences, while others were housed in the barracks of former German soldiers.

I was taken to a displaced persons camp in Feldafing. Refugees continued to stream in. The buildings were packed. Fresh from the horrors of the war, used to seeing the deepest sorrow, I suddenly encountered angels—kind, generous, godly men and women who volunteered at the DP, putting their needs aside to care for these survivors like parents caring for their children. (I even woke up in the morning to sweet voices singing the prayer *"modeh ani"* to the refugees, just as my mother had done for me as a child.) These volunteers bathed them, clothed them, fed them, and brought them back to life. They helped them take their first steps forward.

As for me, I had arrived there barely alive, without a tooth in my mouth to bite down on food. But I was thankful just to have a bed to sleep in, rather than lying on a wooden shelf inside a cubicle stuffed with prisoners, or on freezing cold ground, or a corpse. For years, we had been denied basic dignity. We hadn't held books to read, seen a colorful fruit, or taken a hot shower with soap. We appreciated the simple everyday choices the average person takes for granted—being able to get out of bed in the morning when you want, stepping into the shower by yourself, or even rinsing your face. Year after year, those decisions are all made *for* you; you can't even walk over and turn on a light. And when you need to go out to that bathroom, there's no piece of paper.

Little by little I regained strength, which lifted my mind too. I stayed in the displaced persons camp only a short while, until I could stand. Many fellow survivors in Feldafing were relieved to finally be on their feet, just to look and act like a human being again. I couldn't conceive of being a free man yet having to stay in the confines of a camp. To be sure, it wasn't like the concentration camps, where they handed you a little bit of coffee and some bread—here, they gave us good food—but nevertheless, I couldn't bear it. I was afraid to get used to being cared for by others. I didn't want to have a life of gifts. My gift, I felt, would come straight from G-d. An intense urge was awakened within me to get out of the building, get moving, and to feel like I was being productive. I needed to make up for all the lost time.

One day, I jumped up from bed and walked to the restroom, where I saw something I hadn't seen in years—myself. I gazed at my reflection in the mirror, and I asked in Yiddish, *"Vu ahin zo lich gain?"*—Where should I go now? I had no family, no friends, and no home.

Then I heard a whisper—*go back to the camp.* So I returned to the place where I was liberated in Dachau. There, I saw an American unit. I went over to the guards and tried to speak to them, but nobody understood me. One of them went to get some-one who spoke Yiddish. Turns out it was the same Jewish captain.

"I remember you crying," he said. "Now you're looking good. Go home," he told me. I sat down on the grass with my head buried in my hands. *I have no home,* I thought.

Another officer walked over, bent down, and handed me a bar of Hershey chocolate and a piece of gum, which I put in my pocket.

"Can you find me some work?" I asked the Jewish captain.

"Come back tomorrow," he said. "I'll see what I can do."

The Jewish captain arranged a job for me in the building where the American officers were stationed. He led me to the kitchen, where I met the manager. On the counter in front of me lay a knife, a few sacks of potatoes, and a bin. When I saw that pile of potatoes along with the other vegetables in front of me, I couldn't believe it—that represented real wealth.

"Peel all of these," I was instructed. "Put the raw potatoes in this bin, and then throw the peels in this trash." Easy enough. But as soon as I began cutting the potatoes, I couldn't bring myself to throw away anything, even the peels. So those didn't go into the trash—I stuffed them inside my shirt. And when I pared them, I cut extra-thick slices, leaving some inner vegetable underneath.

When the supervisor came in to check on me, it didn't take long to notice my bloated shirt. He walked over, patted me, and asked me to unbutton my shirt, where he discovered all the peels. He immediately figured I was a thief.

"Stealing! This is called stealing," he said. I couldn't under-stand a word, but I knew what he meant. I also remembered the penalty for picking up any small bit from the mud in the camps, and how my friend Moshe Rappaport had paid with his life.

Shaky, I tried my best to explain—first in German, then in Polish—but he didn't understand. So he went to call in the Jewish captain. The captain brought me to an office with two other soldiers, where he served as my translator.

"Tell me why you stole these," he said to me in Yiddish.

"For the past few years, those peels would have meant a festival for me and my fellow prisoners," I said. "I wanted to save them."

His face filled with compassion as he sighed. "Just peel potatoes and throw away the peels—like we told you," he warned softly.

One of the other men took my misstep more seriously. He held out a brown Bible, motioned for me to put my hand on it, and he prompted me—word by word—to vow that I would never take anything again.

"If we catch you taking any of the food for yourself," the man warned, "you won't work here anymore." They walked me back to the kitchen.

The next day, I was determined to gain their trust. I cut the peels thinner than a piece of tissue paper and put everything in its proper place: the potatoes in the bin and the peels in the trash, just as they had instructed me.

But something caught my eye: Across the room, in the corner of the kitchen, was a table stacked with the most beautifully wrapped packages of pastries—in fact, it was white bread, but we didn't have white bread in Poland—and I couldn't resist. I walked over to the table, checked if anyone was around. With no one in sight, I lifted up a loaf to take a closer look. The next instant, I was hiding under the table, sitting with the loaf on my knees, tearing open the packaging, and gobbling one slice of bread at a time until I had devoured almost an entire loaf. As I reached the last two slices, two men walked in—I was caught.

They brought me up to the same office. "You stole again! We warned you last time—I'm afraid you can't come here anymore."

I broke down in tears. "Cry as much as you want," the man said, "but it won't help. Just tell us why you keep stealing."

"For the past few years," I told them—I must have repeated that phrase three times—"I had a dream, and I had a jealousy."

One of the men laughed. "A jealousy—in such conditions, who were you possibly jealous of?"

I continued, "As we prisoners starved, we sometimes saw S.S. guards feasting. At one point, I had fantasized that if I ever made it out of this war alive, and if I ever saw one loaf of bread, I'd finish every last piece. That was my dream."

"Then what was your jealousy?"

"One spring morning, during a roll call, I watched a small yellow butterfly float through the air and land on the ground right in front of me. I looked down and examined it closely while it flexed its wings over the concrete. When the German officer's boot suddenly approached my space, the butterfly lifted itself and silently glided off in the distance. That butterfly flew away—but I was stuck. I couldn't go anywhere. That was my jealousy!" I cried.

I looked at the men, who stood there speechless, each of their eyes filling with teardrops. They agreed to give me one more chance.

The next day, a tall, stout officer strolled into the kitchen. I noticed that his army uniform had a lot more shiny stars—not just two stripes—so I assumed he was a higher rank. That made me nervous.

He walked straight to me, stopped, and stuck out his hand for me to shake. Still apprehensive to engage a high-ranking officer in any friendly or casual manner (which in the camps was shameful for the officer and spelled punishment for the prisoner), I just stood there with my hands by my side.

Observing my reluctance, he immediately tried to put me at ease. He began speaking to me in Polish. "I heard you're from Radom. My parents came to America from Poland — I was born in Chicago — but we always spoke Polish in the house. Don't be afraid to shake hands with me. It'll make me feel good."

I shook his hand, and then he hugged me.

"You'll be all right," he said.

<hr />

I wanted to lead a normal life. The war was over, I was free and had a job — but I considered myself far from being normal. My mind was wounded and spinning in the wrong places. At that point, there were many directions my life could have taken.

To be sure, I was still careful to observe certain kosher dietary laws, such as not to eat pig's meat, but I had ill feelings for G-d, and plenty of complaints.

Of the 33,000 Jews who had lived in Radom, more than 90 percent were exterminated. From looking on posted lists, I had learned that my mother, Chava, had perished in Auschwitz. My brother Dovid had been sent to Treblinka. None of my uncles, aunts, or cousins remained. Then, a short while afterward I was speaking with some Polish survivors, and discovered the fate of my brothers Sruel and Yankele in Warsaw.

Before the war, Sruel had been friendly with Mordechai Anielewicz, leader of the Jewish Combat Organization. During the Warsaw ghetto uprising, against the wishes of Mary, Sruel began smuggling weapons to the Jews in the ghetto. My baby brother, Yankele (who was then 7), worked as a courier, crawling through the sewers to smuggle weapons. They were both eventually caught and executed.

I still carried haunting images in my head, like that Jewish mother sobbing as she nursed her baby, changing it, wrapping it so delicately, kissing it, and then leaving it on someone else's doorstep. *How could G-d be a bystander?*

As I continued to recuperate in the displaced persons camp, my perspective gradually changed. I watched with amazement how staff cared for the survivors, even teaching them again how to eat, how to sleep, how to behave. I once asked a volunteer in his early 30s: "Do you have parents?"

"Yes, I have parents. I still have my grandparents. They all live in America."

That simple exchange restored my faith in humanity. Their *chesed* (kindness) brought me back. Seeing other young people giving up lots of things to help, you say to yourself: *There must be a G-d. There are still good people in this world. So why can't I too try to live a normal life?*

For so many years my mind and emotions had degenerated; our existence was an animalistic struggle, scavenging to survive. I still felt far from normal, but I resolved to at least *pretend* to be normal. I now had models from which I could observe their daily routines and deeds, noting how normal, refined humans acted and trying to imitate their success. And that power of observation would serve me well for years to come.

Slowly, I regained my footing and built up my confidence. The chance to lead a normal life, however, wouldn't happen for a while—I still had a debt to pay.

CHAPTER 11

"I Don't Want Money for That"

O ne morning, I woke up to two men standing over my bed. They were impeccably dressed in suits. I hadn't seen someone outfitted in such a beautiful suit in years.

They began to inquire about what languages I spoke. I told them I was originally from Poland, that I hadn't gone to school to learn any other languages, but that over the last six years, just from being around prisoners and guards, I had picked up Russian, German, Czech, and Yugoslav.

"You speak good German?" they asked excitedly.

Their enthusiasm startled me. "Are you SD?" I immediately inquired. SD, meaning *Sicherheitsdienst*, was an intelligence-gathering body of Nazi Germany. From my time in the camps, I was familiar with almost every German agency and type of officer.

"No, don't worry," the man replied. "We're Americans, from the United States intelligence service" (though he used the phrase "secret police" while speaking to me in German). "We would like to offer you a job."

"What am I going to have to do?"

"You'll be hunting Nazis."

I didn't know exactly what that meant, but I had lost my entire family and figured that I still had a debt to pay, whatever it involved.

"We will compensate you well for this work—"

"No, I don't want money for that," I said boldly. "Where do you sleep and eat?"

"We have an officers' mess hall."

"Can I get that too? That's all I want," I said.

They gladly agreed.

—➤-◦-◄—

They brought me to their headquarters, where I was introduced to their superior, an older gentleman, who interviewed me and briefed me about the job. The Americans then sent me to a local college for a six-week crash course in English so that I would be able to communicate better with them. They also sent me to a dentist to replace my teeth as best he could. I put on weight and looked good as new.

Then I began training for my job: to mingle amongst Germans and pose as a young Nazi ex-soldier or collaborator trying to flee the country.

I slept in the same place as the other agents; I dined with them. They all treated me warmly, adopted me like their little brother. In addition to their feeling pity, knowing what I'd just endured, I think they respected the fact that I was willing to risk my life again. I had come of age in the midst of a nightmare, and despite the intensity of the jobs they would give me, being around the American officers and feeling that sense of companionship ended up being one of the sweetest, most enjoyable periods in my life.

I couldn't drive, so they gave me a driver, Joe Brovian. Joe and I quickly became friends. He told me that before the war, he had played professional sports for a team in New York—some game with a wooden stick I'd never heard of. The thought of grown men getting paid to run around with a club and a little ball made no sense to me.

The United States intelligence service wanted to know where Nazis were hiding and how they were trying to escape. From having earned the confidence of one of them, they got some information about people to contact.

Joe would drop me around the corner from one of the hideouts they had identified. My mission was to go in with an urgent request—I was trying to get out of Germany and needed the names of people who could help me escape. I would inquire about the best hiding places. The only way you could get that information was if you were recommended by somebody. And you had to be able to speak basic German.

When I arrived at the house, the first obstacle was to be let in. I walked up wearing an SS uniform, which the Americans had given me—to serve as proof, just in case—and a long overcoat. There was always a buffer at the entrance—a peasant or simple-looking civilian—who opened the door.

For example: I knocked. An old lady opened.

"What do you want? Who are you looking for?" she asked.

I told her the name of the person I was looking to speak with. She let me inside and led me down to a basement where two or three men were waiting. My instructions were not to ask any questions—no names or who they were. Those I was mingling with were former *Sicherheitsdienst* men, or they could have been Gestapo, or *Polizei*, all people who might have gleefully sent me to my death.

Once it happened that I was speaking to a guard I recognized from the camps. Fortunately, he didn't recognize me. By that time, I was not a walking skeleton anymore. I'd already put on some healthy weight. My head was no longer shaved; I now wore a thick head of hair. I smelled good, was well groomed, and dressed stylishly.

I pulled out a pack of cigarettes in my pocket, and I handed people cigarettes. One man lit up the cigarettes and poured a bottle of schnapps. I never sat down. We all had a drink, and then got straight to the point. "They're looking for me—how can I be smuggled out from Germany?"

What I needed from them were directions on who to connect with.

"Where would you like to go? South America—Chile, Argentina—or you can go to Australia." I didn't recognize some of the cities they suggested, but after hearing the list, I'd give them an answer.

Then they'd tell me where to find the next person—go to Landsberg, Augsburg, Bremerhaven, and so forth—and which railroad station or airport to find the contact.

"When you get there, there'll be somebody taking care of you, but you will never see that person a second time." In other words, I was connected, and then immediately disconnected from them. And if one came back to that house a few days later, there would be no sign of the men I spoke with.

I'd stay in the basement talking 15 minutes. One Nazi salute and you got out. During those conversations, I had to remain ice cold, completely composed—it's easy to spot a person who's lying or fearful—and if I showed any signs of nervousness, I might not have made it out. But I did not go in there with fear. As far as I was concerned, I'd already survived the worst. Now was my time—and I was no longer afraid of anybody. From then on, even in America when I made a good living, I took lots of chances with my life.

Me dressed in my uniform.

With Joe Brovian (right).

After we were successful in catching some Nazis, I also testified as a witness before the International Military Tribunal. When I showed up at the trial, I expected to see these war criminals being led into the courtroom sheepishly, and then promptly convicted. Instead they entered proudly, dressed in slick attire, accompanied by the best defense attorneys that money could buy.

These lawyers came well prepared.

"Yes, I recognize that officer," I'd answer, describing, for example, how the man lined up prisoners and thrust his knife through their stomach. Or I'd relate another crime, such as how one evening, that man came down with his friend from the guard tower, pulled out his pistol, and shot four prisoners—for fun.

After I finished identifying the soldier, they'd begin to interrogate me: "According to our records, you weighed 69 pounds when you were liberated. You couldn't stand for a roll call. You were sick, had typhus. In such a state, are you telling me that you can remember when and who committed these crimes?"

I was not prepared for their cross-examination—going in, I had thought the criminals would be the ones to be questioned closely—but I did not panic or hesitate. "Hitler took everything from me—my whole family—but one thing he didn't take from me is my mind and my memory," I told them. "And I know what I saw. Whenever I observed someone committing an atrocity, I can tell you the face, the exact place, and the time of day that it happened—now direct your inquiry to him!" From that moment, I refused to answer any more of their questions—I had already identified the Nazis, confirmed their crimes, and they had enough prosecution witnesses.

But after those Nazis had been sentenced, before they were hung, it was my turn to ask the questions—and the American military officials obliged. I took the rope from the hangman, held it in my hand, and looked this sadist in the eye. I did not grab the rope because I intended to do anything with it—I would never get my hands dirty in that way—but I wanted to show that SS guard across from me that he was not such a big man anymore. In fact, he trembled with fear—but I never cried when I was getting beaten.

"Tell me," I said to the Nazi. "How could you be out all day long, committing the crimes that you committed, pulling children and old people into the ovens by their feet, sticking your army dagger through people's mouths—and then come home at night, take off your jacket, and kiss your wife and children and dare to say the words 'I love you'?"

I put this question to a few of these monsters before their death, and most answered with an excuse. The most shocking response was "If the Fuhrer had ordered me to do the same thing to them, I would have done it too."

I then handed the rope back to the hangman. "By my orders, you can hang him."

That's for my family!

CHAPTER 12

Her Skirt Was Made from a Blanket

At the displaced persons camps, new life was beginning to blossom. Food was still scarce, but culture and education became vital to the survivors in their attempt to move forward. Hope filled the air as people were in a hurry to escape their past and return to a stable life, or at least the appearance of one. In only a short time, refugees established sports clubs, education for children; there were clothing workshops, art activities, film screenings, and more.

I heard that a Yiddish play, *The Dybbuk*, was playing at the center in Feldafing. I went there, still dressed in an American officer's uniform. The room was packed with people, and the lights were off. As I scouted around for an empty seat, I noticed a group of five young ladies seated in the back row and looking in my direction.

Two of them walked over to me. One offered me her seat; the other said, "I'll take your coat."

She held my coat for the entire show. When the film finished and the lights went on, I stood up and went over to take my coat. We began talking.

"What's your name?" I asked.

"Esther."

"How old are you?"

"Seventeen."

Dear Lord, I thought. *An 11-year-old child when the war broke out, now likely an orphan…*

I noticed that her skirt was made from a blanket and her blouse from a bedsheet. But she had managed to do it tastefully. She was put together, and her hair was gorgeous. I immediately wanted to say something to compliment her. What came out was "I like your outfit."

"Really?" she answered innocently. "I have more sets at home."

"Where do you live?"

She told me she stayed at the displaced persons camp with a cousin. She shared a room with four girls.

The next day, I came to visit her there. I thanked her for holding my jacket, and the other girl for giving me her seat. Soon after we began talking, Esther went to the drawer. "See," she said, pulling out a pile of clothes made from bedding, "I told you I have some more."

I told her, "I'll see you in a few days."

During that time, merchandise was limited and most retail operations had shut down; you weren't able to walk into stores and buy dresses. But I knew a merchant who traveled to Italy. "Kohl," I said, "I need a favor: When you go down there, get me some nice material for dresses." I handed him a bag of coffee and a carton of cigarettes in trade. A few days later, he returned with seven pieces of fine fabric. I took the fabrics to a seamstress and had five dresses made for Esther, along with some undergarments. I also bought her some shoes, which I paid for with coffee and sugar.

For the next few weeks, I visited Esther. Whenever I came, I brought things from the officers' mess hall—things she didn't have, like fresh fruits and chocolate. And every time I gave her something, she'd take my hand and kiss it. Then I kissed her forehead.

We talked about our experiences in the war, memories of the people close to us, our homes. She was the daughter of a distinguished family from the Polish town of Krzepice. Her father had served as the community president. Like me, she'd lost her entire family.

━━▶‣·◦·◄‣━━

The American officers were taking a trip to Paris. "Do you want to come along?" one of them asked me. G-d works in mysterious ways, and the moment I heard the word "Paris," a vision was implanted in my brain, taking me back to my childhood in Poland when I used to collect the stamps from letters received from relatives abroad. I saw the address on letters from my sister—34 Rue Le Marais, Paris 5. I immediately agreed to come along.

There were no banks in Europe during that time. Everything was kept under people's mattresses. I put all my cigarettes and money in a suitcase. I went to the DP camp and told Esther, "I'm going to Paris. Can I leave this case with you until I come back?"

"Of course," she said. "I'll take good care of it for you."

All I brought with me to Paris was six cartons of cigarettes. When we arrived in Paris, I went to the counter of the Hotel Ritz and offered the man two cartons of cigarettes in exchange for a room. He agreed.

That evening, I went to visit the address I remembered. I asked the concierge if the family still lived there.

"Moshe Golebiowski was taken to Auschwitz," she said sadly, "but Madame Nannette is still alive."

"Can I speak with her?"

"I'll take you to see her tomorrow morning."

The next morning, she brought me to a diner on Rue de Turbigo, where we met a woman in her thirties with dark hair. I greeted her and sat down. I was not yet sure it was my sister and whether she would recognize me — I was only a boy when she left, and I was dressed in an American uniform.

We just looked at each other. First test: I spoke to her in Yiddish. "Madame Golebiowski, I believe we're related — I am a cousin from America. Can I ask you a few questions about your family in Poland?"

"Certainly," she answered in Yiddish.

I asked her father's name, her mother's name, about her siblings. As she answered, I realized — *it was my sister!* I had lost all hope of seeing any relatives, and now my only sister was in front of me. The joy was indescribable, a surreal sense of witnessing someone coming back to life from the grave. But I held myself back from telling her who I was, lest she faint from the sudden shock or suffer a heart attack.

We talked for half a day. Eventually, I leaned over and told her, "Enough is enough — let me tell you who I am. You remember your brother Sruel?" I asked.

"Yes."

"Your younger brother Dovid, your brother Itzik?" (She never saw our youngest sibling, so I didn't ask about him.)

"Yes, of course I do," she said, confused.

"Well, I'm your little brother, Itzik!"

We began sobbing together, and embraced. She told me about her life in Paris before the war, how she and her husband, Moshe, had worked in the restaurant business and had a fine Parisian lifestyle. They had a baby girl together, Malka. Then one day, while crossing the street together near the Place de la

République, they noticed a unit of police officers in the town square. Two officers stopped them and asked Moshe for his identification papers. As they were arresting him, my sister fled, darted across the street, and hid in the bathroom of a nearby café. She waited there for a few hours before making her way home safely. There she destroyed all her personal documents and packed her bags. Friends in the complex replaced the name on the apartment with that of a non-Jewish resident, while my sister and her young daughter were hidden in the apartment of the concierge.

After the war she learned of her husband's murder. By pure chance, she bumped into a survivor she recognized from Radom. He had known Moshe in the camps, and recounted the bitter episode of how her husband had hidden a piece of bread in his barrack while he went out to work. Upon returning, he discovered that his only food had been snatched by a fellow prisoner. Moshe confronted him, and the two men came to blows. A German officer stood nearby and watched the scuffle in amusement, letting them fight it out before shooting them both.

The next day she took me to a parochial school. She told me to wait, and came out with an 8-year-old child. "This is my daughter, Malka."

At first, Malka was startled to see her mother with a young man wearing an American uniform, but we soon overcame that hesitation.

We rented a one-room apartment on Rue du Fer à Moulin, and my sister, niece, and I spent two full days together catching up and reminiscing about our lost family members and childhood memories. We even went to a photographer in Paris to capture the moment. It was an unforgettable day, but it would be decades until I saw my sister again. She eventually remarried, and we were reunited in 1965 when the couple flew to visit us in Dallas.

Nannette, me, and Malka, 1945.

When I returned from Paris, I went to the DP to see Esther and pick up my suitcase from her. When I came in, her friends told me, "You know, for two weeks, Esther didn't leave the house; she sat on your suitcase the entire time."

I looked at her, and it hit me. *I feel alone in the world. She is by herself. For months I've been visiting her, and the only kiss I ever gave her was on her forehead. This is the girl for me!*

"Esther," I said, "you don't have a soul in the world. I don't have anyone. Let's get married and build a home together!"

I dressed up in my nicest clothes. Jewelry was one of the easier things for me to acquire, so I found a nice gold band and put a precious stone on it, and we had a small wedding ceremony at the end of 1945 in a little *beis midrash* in Munich. We invited about 30 survivors. The rabbi was also a survivor, a young man we knew from the displaced persons camp. We had *lekach* (honey cake) and *bronfen* (whiskey), herring, and bread rolls. It was simple but warm—with a lot of crying, bittersweet tears from the present joy mixed with an acute awareness of the void within a wedding celebration without parents, grandparents, or any loved ones.

After suffering so much destruction in our world, we now had the chance to create new life and to bring children into this world. That day was the start of a beautiful, harmonious life together—50 years of marriage.

Our wedding day.

Esther and me in Germany.   *With a friend at the DP camp.*

Me walking with the burgermeister in Munich
at the yearly commemoration of liberation.

CHAPTER 13

"By Someone Else's Hand"

An American GI was allotted four cartons of cigarettes a month—that meant he could smoke a carton a week— but since I wouldn't accept pay, they gave me six cartons. On top of that, individual soldiers would sometimes give me packs of cigarettes as gifts. I didn't smoke. So although I didn't have greenbacks, I accumulated cartons of cigarettes, which I could exchange on the black market for coffee, produce, high-priced liquor like cognac, chocolates, and whatever interesting goods were available.

Then I opened a little store in downtown Munich. From the outside, you couldn't tell it was a store—I needed to be able to pack up and move on short notice—but inside there were plenty of goods.

In no time at all, I was doing well, well enough that Esther and I moved to a seaside villa in a small resort town, Seeshaupt. I hired two young Germans to work in my store, Heinz and Willem, though with the type of work we did, I never knew whether those were their real names. Their job was to ensure my security, along with bringing in coveted merchandise and recommending customers to my store. In a flash, my world had been drastically transformed. I had become a hustler, operating in the center of Munich, dealing in jewelry and earning as my father had done, with two Germans working for *me*.

Fresh after the war, chaos and disillusionment filled the air. People were coming and going to all different places at a rapid pace. Most refugees I knew, those skilled enough to find work, didn't intend to settle in Germany. But everyone needed to eat, and many were prepared to do just about anything. My two friends from the Dachau concentration camp ran their own underground businesses. The Austrian fellow, who was an expert in printing, operated an outfit forging documents and was making a fortune. At that time, everything was bought on ration cards, including food and clothing. He produced counterfeit ration cards. People looking to move to other countries came to him, and he'd make them into almost any type of professional they desired by creating "official" medical diplomas, degrees, and other dubious documentation.

The three of us made a pact: When the time came to go our separate ways, we would never speak to anyone about anything we had seen or done together. Eventually, the rabbi's son moved to Israel, and the Austrian moved to Australia. I never had contact with them again.

<hr />

One day, a young Jewish man walked into my store and introduced himself as Menachem Begin. He was also from Poland and was now living in Palestine, which was under British mandate. We spoke in Yiddish for a while. He asked about my background and admired an MG42 (German machine gun) that I displayed behind the counter and some hard-to-find items that I had in the store.

Then I discovered the purpose of his visit. "We're going to have our own country one day," he told me. "We could really use people like you over there."

At that time, there were plenty of survivors to choose from. Ships from German ports smuggled these young men over to Palestine to help fight for independence. I was just getting comfortable, was busy trying to forget the violence of the war, and I had no intention of going anywhere.

I was blunt in my rejection: "Listen, Menachem. You seem like a good man, but I just survived years in hell. I'm doing okay where I am."

He gave me a slight grin and seemed to understand.

"But perhaps I can be of assistance to you," I continued. "Come back here tomorrow evening."

I went to work quickly. I knew where the warehouses were that housed weapons seized from the German prisoners. I approached Heinz and Willem, the two Germans who were working in my store, and told them I had an urgent job. The first thing was to send them out to the British zone. They brought back two trucks and painted them green, like army trucks.

Next, they lifted some American license plates and put them on the trucks. They drove to a base in Augsburg. Two guards stood at each entrance. To get in, we had to offer more than cigarettes—Germans could be bribed with one carton of cigarettes, but not these guys; four bottles of five-star French cognac did the job.

They drove to the warehouse, handed more cigarettes to the warehouse guards. The guards loaded some pistols, rifles, grenades, or whatever ammo they could get onto the truck. We took it to Bremerhaven.

When Menachem returned the next evening, I told him to meet my workers there. What happened to those truckloads afterward, I have no idea. But I felt like I had done my part to help my people.

I would see Menachem Begin again many years later when I visited Israel with my wife. He remembered me, and received us in royal fashion.

⟫-◦-⟪

In 1946, my uncle from Texas had sent me papers to come to America. I didn't want to go. I knew that as an immigrant arriving in America, you'd have to roll up your sleeves and go to work right away. And as an immigrant in a foreign country, barely speaking the language, and without anything in your pocket, you'd already be in debt from the onset. So I delayed it.

We stayed in Germany until '47, and then I put it off again. At the end of '47, I was a rich man by local standards. In 1948 we had our first child, a baby girl, Lotty. We lived in a nice villa. Then they changed the currency. So I and my poor wife were back to the beginning.

In 1949 the American consul sent us a notification that basically said: "Either you go to America or we will cancel the visa—because you have put it off four times." So Esther and I went to the American embassy to obtain papers for the trip.

As we were walking into the office, I saw a familiar face walking out. It was Heil Friedman, the Jewish officer who had worked in the Radom camp, walked around with a whip, and beat prisoners, sometimes just for fun. I stood by the door and stared at him. He immediately recognized me and recoiled. Then he came to shake my hand, as if we were old friends.

I did not oblige. "Where are you moving to, Heil?" I asked.

"I'm going to Sydney, Australia," he answered. "I'm so happy to leave this dreadful country."

I moved closer and looked into his eyes. "Do you remember

what you did to us in the camps, Heil?" I said, while clasping his forearm.

I felt him begin to quiver. One shout from me to the police and he'd likely be finished—they'd pick him up and he'd never see daylight again.

Instead, a rare spirit of mercy entered at that moment, and I just shook my head, turned to my wife behind me, and declared in Yiddish: "Let him fall by someone else's hand—not mine."

I released my grip. Heil Friedman hurriedly walked out the door and eventually moved to Australia. Almost 50 years later, when I visited Sydney on vacation, I looked him up out of curiosity but kept my distance.

This is the day that the Lord made;
we shall exult and rejoice in it.

— Psalms 118:24

CHAPTER 14
Welcome to Greenville

My wife and I, along with our baby daughter, Lotty, traveled from Munich to the seaport in Bremerhaven, where we took a ship to New Orleans. The ship was filled with Jewish immigrant families. When we stopped in New Orleans, the local Jewish committee was prepared to house us. Their staff picked us up and took us to a building. We congregated on the second floor. I went to look around downstairs. Outside the building there was a little restaurant and marketplace.

I had brought some American currency, which I had saved. For a dime, I bought two small bottles of Coca-Cola. Then I purchased four hamburgers, some oranges, and bananas, and carried the bags upstairs to Esther and the baby.

Well, on a shipload of immigrants, all eyes are watching you — even after you get off. As soon as I walked back inside, a young Jewish man came running over, asking, "Wow! Where did you get that?"

Thinking it best not to reveal the details, I told him, "A good-hearted American bought it for me."

"America is good," he exclaimed.

<hr/>

From New Orleans we went to Tyler, Texas. My uncle and aunt came to pick us up in a big blue Cadillac and took us to their home in Greenville, Texas. The town of Greenville is situated in the heart of the Texas Blackland Prairies, 45 minutes northeast of Dallas. As soon as I arrived in the States, I had already begun the habit of learning more English by reading every street sign I could. On the main street in the downtown district, between the train station and the bus station, there was a big sign welcoming visitors to Greenville that read "the Blackest Land, the Whitest People." I couldn't yet figure out what that one meant.

Being an immigrant Jew in South Texas seemed to promise intimidating encounters. Yet since the 1870s, Jewish merchants had played an integral role in the cash crop economy that developed in the city of Greenville. Jewish merchants, observing the growing population of farmers in need of dry goods and various supplies, set up stores to meet the demands. The success of the cotton industry in Greenville provided many families ample income. And soon, Jewish merchants started selling more luxurious goods.

Before the war, Sam Swartz, a tailor, had married my mother's sister, Basha (Becky), in Poland. My father had helped them to acquire the travel tickets for the initial journey to America and some extra pocket money. They went through Ellis Island and wound up in Greenville, where my uncle opened up a small retail business. He had a tailor shop where he did alterations, and he housed the family in the back of the store. I had heard that if not for his wife, Sam would have likely remained in that little room with a needle and thread. But she was a clever lady.

"You don't need to do this type of work forever," she encouraged him. "We can make better money without the needle." From that tailor shop they opened up a thrift store, which they closed after two years, then opened a dry goods store. Swartz then bought a neighboring building, allowing him to expand his clothing inventory. Eventually they opened the Sam Swartz Department Store, across from the courthouse. It sold high-end clothing and attracted better clientele. The local newspaper identified Swartz's store as an example of the city's development, suggesting that "the store has literally grown up with Greenville." Later, their son, Max, opened a store in Dallas, and others in Hillsboro, Bonham, Athens, and Paris, Texas. In short, by the time I arrived, the family was well established.

They received us warmly and offered me a job working at their store in downtown Greenville. To my wife and me, their home seemed like a castle. Everything was brand new, finely crafted furniture, and exquisitely decorated rooms. They showed us to the guest room where we'd be staying. My young wife, who had been separated from her parents at 11 years old, thought we'd won the lottery. After they left us to unpack in the bedroom, she clutched my hand in excitement. "What a beautiful place your uncle and aunt have given us."

How two minds can look at the same picture and see differently. I felt uneasy in such plush accommodation. "My dear child," I said to her in Yiddish. "I love you, and I love our baby. The room is indeed beautiful, but it's not ours. It's only a temporary place—for you to relax for a while—until we can get our own."

I reclined on the bed to rest but could barely stay still for 30 minutes. My head was spinning. We'd survived the war. Now we faced a different style of survival. True, America offered new opportunities, but also so many things I had never seen or heard about. People spoke a different language, ate different foods, and had a different culture. Doubt began to run through my mind. *Where am I? What's happened? What will it be?*

I stood up. "I'm going to go down to see where my uncle's store is," I told Esther.

I walked out the front door, stood on the sidewalk in front of the house for a minute, then headed toward town. People in Greenville, Texas, had good ol' Southern hospitality. As I was walking, a farmer stopped with his truck.

"Where you goin', boy?"

"Sam Swartz store," I answered with a clear accent.

"Hey, where you from?"

"I've just come from Germany."

"Hop in."

I climbed into the truck, and he brought me to my uncle's store. I walked inside and looked around. I was used to tight storefronts and classic European architecture. Here, everything was operating on a grander scale. The building was huge; there were extensive areas with separate departments for jewelry, suits, casual clothes, and luggage. Each department had managers, clerks, and salespeople, while my uncle and his son-in-law, Herb Rosas, a lawyer from New York, supervised the entire store.

Impressed by the operation, I walked around, observing the salespeople helping customers, and mentally recorded my first line: "May I help you, sir?" I practiced that a few times.

Just then, my aunt pulled up in her Cadillac, parked in front of the store, and rushed inside to where I was standing. "*Meshugener*—why did you run down to the store?" she asked.

"I wanted to see where Uncle works," I answered.

"You just arrived here — get in the car. You need to rest."
She pulled me outside and drove me home right away.

⸻•⸻

After a day in the house, I said, "I'm ready to go to work." So I went back to the store, this time with a wooden pencil and a yellow pad.

When Sam's son-in-law saw me with that, he made a sly remark to my uncle: "This young man's not coming to work — he's coming to learn the business."

Then he started up with me. "You're not going to school, you know."

"Yes," I answered. "But I want to learn how you say all these clothes in English."

I stood by, observing the store, eager to make a sale. Never bashful, I grabbed a customer and parroted the line I'd learned a few days ago. "May I help you, sir? "

"Where are your BVDs?" he asked.

A word I'd never heard — but I didn't want to let the customer know that. "Wait a second," I said. "I'll be right back."

Moving quickly around the store, I examined all the signs above the stands, sounding out the words in my head — no sign of BVDs. Meanwhile, the man was watching me and growing impatient. After a few minutes, I walked back to him.

"Sir, I'm sorry. I've just moved here from Europe — can you tell me: What's a BVD?"

"Union suits!" he said. "You know, like long undergarments."

He told me his size, I found it for him, took it over to the register, and they took the money. That was my first sale.

A few days passed; everything was smooth and fine, until one day, a truck arrived with some wrapping paper and paper bags. Everybody went out and carried it in, so I did too. All of a sudden, I was left alone. I went inside. "Listen," I told them. "Either everybody does it together or nobody does it."

Deep in my mind I said, *If my uncle's been down here, made a fortune—this is not really the place for me.* So I was always looking for another opportunity.

A short while later I found it. A fire broke out across the parking lot, in a small store that sold animal feed, right next door to another Jewish owner, Rosenberg. I went there to see what was going on.

When I heard the owners mention that they planned to close, I immediately offered to buy that little store. I had recently emerged from the abyss in Germany and didn't conceive that some might view it as business rivalry. I just figured it was better than working for my uncle. At least I wouldn't be taking orders from anyone.

But as soon as my uncle heard about my offer, he decided I was up to no good. "Greenville is not the place for you to work," he said. I was unofficially evicted from town.

CHAPTER 15
Quick Sales

"Here," said my uncle as he scribbled an address on a piece of paper, then handed it to me. "Go down to the depot, go to Dallas, and see my son, Max—he has a job for you."

Max lived in Dallas, Texas, where he ran a chain of eight clothing stores. I hadn't yet been to Dallas, and I didn't know what a depot was—but I was going to find out. I walked through Greenville looking for signs that read "depot." Finally I stopped a guy and asked him, "Where is the depot?"

"Oh, that's the Greyhound bus station, right down the street," he said, pointing me in the direction.

I found it and bought a ticket to Dallas, Texas.

Arriving at the bus station in Dallas, I went from Jackson Street to the intersection of Elm and Pearl, where my cousin's office building stood. There were no cars coming, so I walked across the street. Suddenly, I heard the loud buzz of a machine. I turned around and saw a police motorcycle with flashing lights, gunning the engine as he sped toward me.

The policeman stepped off his bike and strolled over to me, as I stood alarmed.

"You know what you did?" he asked.

"Here to see Max Swartz — the fourth floor," I answered in Yiddish, figuring that speaking a foreign language was my safest way out of any offense.

"You don't speak English?"

I shook my head. The police officer began pointing to the lights and the crosswalk signals, trying to explain jaywalking to an immigrant, while I continued to emphasize my confusion.

Meanwhile, three Jewish merchants who worked in the building — Morris Reisberg, who owned a dry goods store; Joe Epoie, who sold security uniforms; and Oscar Utay, who ran a pawnshop — observed the scene from their office windows. One after the other stepped outside to offer assistance. I now had three translators.

The policeman grew irritated. "Y'all go back to work," he snapped, "I can handle this myself."

He looked at me. "See — red light? No go! Green light? Go. Good?"

The officer then kindly walked me across the street and helped me find Max Swartz's place.

My cousin was sitting at his desk working busily. He spoke to me for a few minutes, all the while barely lifting his head as he flipped through documents and jotted notes in his ledger. He mentioned that I could work for him at the clothing store in Hillsboro. The only thing was, he explained, I'd need to stay in Hillsboro during the week and return to my family in Greenville on Fridays.

After a few minutes, he ripped off a sheet from the yellow notepad on his desk and jotted the store address. "Go back to the depot and take the bus to Hillsboro, Texas." He didn't ask me if I had eaten yet that day, or if I had any money for a ticket — thank

G-d I still had some change in my pocket. I went back to the same depot and bought a ticket to Hillsboro.

⇒►-0-◄⇐

I arrived at Max's store in Hillsboro, Texas, just before 6 o'clock. On the sidewalk in the front of the store there stood a young man.

"You the fellow that Max sent?" he said.

"Yes, that's me," I answered. "I'm supposed to start working here."

"Good. I'll see you at 8 tomorrow morning." With that, he turned off the lights, jerked the door closed, locked it, and walked away to his car.

Now, I knew I had to spend the night in Hillsboro, but I had no clue where to go, where to eat, and what to do next. I walked around until I saw a place selling food. I bought two hamburgers for 25 cents each and a Coca-Cola for a nickel. I sat down, ate, and then went around town looking for a hotel.

The first hotel I found was $2 a night.

"I just came from Germany, and I don't have too much money," I told the man behind the counter. "But I'll be coming down here to work each week. Can you help me out?"

"How long are you going to be staying?" he asked.

They hadn't yet told me how long I'd be working in Hillsboro, but it was just as easy to quote the hotel clerk a long time—maybe he'd give me a deal. Sure enough, he gave me the room at a bargain rate of $1 a night, $30 a month. I was relieved —until I opened the door to the room. There was no air conditioner, not even a fan, and the Texas heat and humidity were high that day. Weary from all the walking and traveling, I collapsed onto the hot, hard mattress. The room felt like a sauna. I took a deep breath and attempted to fall asleep as the sweat ran all over my body. After tossing around in discomfort for a few minutes, I stood up, walked to the restroom, and turned on the water in the bathtub. I climbed in and slept there the entire night.

⟹▷•◁⟸

I had been working in Hillsboro for only a few months when I discovered that my cousin's business there was going bankrupt. One day, a group of men showed up at the door. They were representatives from K. Wolens's department store. The Wolenses were a prominent Jewish family in Corsicana, Texas, who then owned dozens of stores in small towns around the state. The stores were founded in 1898 by Kalman Wolens—"Mr. K," as he was fondly called—who had immigrated to Corsicana from Poland, via Chicago, with his wife, Ida, three young sons, and one daughter.

Three Wolens brothers entered our store in Hillsboro along with some of their business managers. I was tickled to learn that the brothers spoke Yiddish. They mingled with Max in the front of the store while the managers were assigned to take inventory of the store. I didn't know what "taking inventory" meant, but if you can write, I can follow.

As the managers went around to each table with a pen recording all the items, I strode right after them with my own journal. When, for example, they counted 30 pairs of pants marked $8.99, they would write $3—the price they'd buy it for—and whatever prices and names they wrote down, I copied down in Yiddish. The only change I made was to round off the numbers; even money was always easier for me. When we finished the inventory, I had totaled $34,000 worth of goods.

That night, we all went out for dinner to a Greek restaurant. I sat by a separate table with some of the managers. But I was close enough to overhear that the Wolens brothers were offering to buy the store for $18,000, lock, stock, and barrel.

During the meal, I pulled Max aside, saying, "Listen, from what I've seen, you've got $34,000 worth of goods. If you accept their offer, you'll be giving away your merchandise and your money…Don't sell it to them! Let me buy a share of the store from you instead."

"Oh, you have that kind of money?" he asked with a smile.

"No, but I guarantee you I can get it for you within a week." I knew that with a quick liquidation sale, we'd make twice what the Wolens brothers were offering him.

"Well, I need to have the money now," Max said to me. We went back and forth for a while. After dinner, he called his father in Greenville and told him all that had happened. "Don't make any deals with anyone yet," Sam instructed Max, "but listen carefully to what Itzik says — he seems to be shrewd, like his father was."

So Max told the Wolenses to give him a day to think about it.

———————

In the end, my cousin decided not to sell the store, neither to the Wolens brothers nor to me. But he did take my advice about conducting a quick sale. When I showed up for work Monday morning, lines of customers were waiting outside. The manager opened the door, and everybody ran in. The store was buzzing. People began grabbing merchandise, loading it on their arms.

For the first 30 minutes I scanned the scene. I saw people walking around a crowded store, their arms full of merchandise, while the manager was just waiting in the corner. I had never seen such commotion. I figured half the stuff would get sold and the other half shoplifted. *I'm going to use my system now,* I said to myself.

So whenever I saw a customer with an armful of goods, I walked over to him, picked up the pile of merchandise, and hurried him to the register. I then handed everything to the cashier to ring up. We put it in a bag and stapled it — and let him out through the back door.

When the manager saw what I was doing, he came charging through the aisle. "I'm going to throw you out of here," he screamed. "You're going to run off our business."

"What's wrong?" I asked him.

"This is not Europe. In America we handle people politely! Give the customer time to make up their mind."

"You know what a thief is?" I asked.

"Yes."

"Well, if you just leave the people in the store like this, half the clothes will be taken."

He shook his index finger and gave me a quick death stare before dashing off to assist a customer.

When evening approached, my main concern was how much we had made that day. My plan was working: In only three days, we took in around $17,000 from sales and still had plenty of merchandise on the stands and in the storage room.

Every two weeks I received $25. But for Christmas Max gave me a bonus $20. I didn't know then what a bonus was, but I knew how much we'd made in that liquidation sale — and that didn't seem fair. I held my peace for the time being. On Friday, I went back to Greenville, Texas, to spend the weekend as usual with my wife and daughter. Monday morning, I didn't go to work in Hillsboro. Instead, I took the bus to Elm and Pearl in Dallas, walked upstairs, and marched into Max Swartz's office.

"Why aren't you at the store?" Max said.

"I want to get something straightened out," I told him. "I just came from Europe, and I'm grateful to Uncle and you for giving me a job. But if you remember, you wanted to sell the store for $18,000. I told you not to, to keep it with me and I'll see that you get your money plus more. You took in close to $17,000 in the first three days — and we still have a store full of merchandise. Am I going to see anything from this?"

"I'll tell you what," he said, sounding quite savvy. "April 15 is when we pay taxes. After that, when we get through with all the accounts, you'll probably come out with big money."

I felt he was playing with my patience, making me wait several months, and that he was taking advantage of me. *The money is going to be with you, and I'm going to be the guy who did all the work to make it?* But if you see the situation coming, you can handle it in a pleasant way. I left him on good terms but never went back to work there.

⎯⎯⎯⎯•◦•⎯⎯⎯⎯

My next stint was at Zale Corporation — another family connection.

Zale Corporation began in 1924 in Wichita Falls, Texas, when Morris Zale, William Zale, and Ben Lipshy opened their first Zales Jewelers store. They were sharp entrepreneurs and implemented a credit plan that let customers pay "a penny down and a dollar a week" for jewelry and other merchandise. Their business was successful, and they expanded to a total of 12 stores in Oklahoma and Texas by 1941.

In 1946, Zales Jewelers moved its headquarters from Wichita Falls to Dallas. Sydney Lipshe, a partner of Zale, was married to my uncle Sam's daughter, Molly. When he heard things didn't work out in Hillsboro, he offered me a job.

Working at a jewelry store seemed like more respectable work, and an area I was familiar with. I showed up to the store on Cliff and Jefferson Street for my first day of work, dressed in one of my tailored suits from Germany. There were two sales-ladies and a manager. The manager walked over to greet me. He was a squat man in his mid-30s, with a slight belly under his big blue patterned tie.

"You the young man from Europe?" he asked.

"Yes, I'm Itzik."

"Nice to meet you," he said. "I'm Steve." Wasting no time, he walked over to the showcases and called, "Come on over here —let me show you what you can do."

He sprayed a few squirts of Windex glass cleaner in four strategic points on the surface of one of the showcases, grabbed a rag, and began spreading it across the surface with strong sweep-ing strides, then dried it using circular motions. He put his head down to examine the case for any overlooked spots before con-tinuing to the next case. As soon as he finished wiping down two, he stopped abruptly, turned around, and handed me the spray and two clean rags.

"Clean 'em all, just like that," he said.

"Sir, with all due respect," I said, "my father never did that type of work, and I am not supposed to do that type of work."

He looked at me angrily. He walked behind the counter, picked up the phone, and dialed my cousin-in-law Sydney.

"You know that boy you sent me, the one from concentra-tion camp, well, he don't want to wipe this table—says he's not going to get his hands dirty."

"Have pity on the young man," I overheard Sydney saying. "He just survived the war. Give him time to get adjusted."

So I hung around for the day.

That evening, just before closing, a young couple walked in to buy an engagement ring. The two ladies who worked in the store brought out different diamonds to show them while the manager stood close by. The man and his fiancée looked through case after case, but couldn't find anything she liked even though the saleswomen worked hard, enthusiastically presenting different engagement sets.

I was always anxious to close a deal, and never shy. I had an idea. When nobody was paying attention, I took the tray with four sets of diamonds away from the showcase and walked into the back room. I polished the diamonds with a strong polish until they shone—something I had learned well from watching my father—then put them into different boxes.

I brought the tray out to the main room. When it looked as though the couple was ready to walk out the door, I stepped forward and said, "Excuse me? My name is Itzik. I just came here from Europe, and I have with me some beautiful new diamonds. If you would sit down for a minute—just to take a look—I'll be happy to show them to you."

They nodded.

I opened up the case, and the light from the newly polished stones was striking. The woman customer's eyes immediately lit up. Without paying much attention to the details of the diamond, she exclaimed, "Oh, my G-d. Look how beautiful."

The man immediately grabbed one of the rings and put it on his fiancée's finger.

"Oh, it's so pretty."

We sold it for $399. I looked on proudly as the salespeople wrapped it up.

But as soon as the customers left the store, the manager walked over and reprimanded me, reminiscent of the episode in Hillsboro.

"What do you think you're doing?"

What am I, a criminal or something? I thought. *I just made a sale!*

He called up Sydney again. "This guy is going to ruin your business. He took over the customers, sat them down, and told them I don't know what. They sat there hypnotized."

Then I heard silence.

"Yes, he sold it," said the manager. He handed me the phone.

"What happened?" Sydney asked. He was nice enough and listened to me.

"Well," I explained, "the two women here couldn't sell the ring. The manager didn't sell it. So I took a case to the back room, polished up some diamonds like you polish your shoes. I brought it back out. Now they shine like a million dollars!"

"Keep up the good work, Itzik, and I'll make *you* the manager soon," Sydney told me.

I had no intention of taking the other man's job. Neither did the manager: When I showed up to work the next day, he again handed me a rag to clean the showcases. I walked to the back room where I'd hung my coat, put it on, and walked out. That was the last time I would work for anybody else.

CHAPTER 16
Make It a Good Day

Dallas is a big city; Greenville is a small town — and they didn't want me working in Greenville anyway. So I told my relatives we were moving to Dallas.

Itzik Rzepkowicz was a hard name for Americans to pronounce. Before we left Greenville, I went to the Hunt County courthouse with my wife, and we paid $12 each to change our names. We were now Jack and Edna Repp.

In those years, before crime increased there, Dallas' most prominent Jewish community was in South Dallas. The neighborhood was thriving. I hired a real estate agent to take me around. As soon as he showed me an apartment and I recognized the names of some other tenants — Levi the plumber lived downstairs, Siegel the liquor store owner upstairs, and Glazer, who ran a large wholesale liquor distribution, owned the building — I rented the vacant three-bedroom apartment upstairs.

My next task was to find a space to operate a little dry-goods store. I found one at 2715 Second Avenue. It was only 1,800 square feet, had an evaporative cooler for the summer, and a little heater for the winter. My storefront was adjacent to Sim's Flowers. The owner and his brother, Tom, lived in the back of their store. Now, Tom got a kick out of unscrewing the water pump from the square box that went into my store. Every so often, when I arrived in the morning to turn it on, nothing came out.

Then, in the afternoon, when it was sometimes around 104 degrees outside, I would feel so hot in my store that I'd walk next door to their shop to cool off near the floral refrigerator. When Tom would see me, he'd start laughing. I never knew why. Finally, one day he said, "I'll fix it for you." He walked outside, and screwed the pump back in.

During the short time that I worked in Hillsboro prior to moving to Dallas, I had learned everything I needed to know about operating a clothing store. I was familiar with all of the brands; all I needed now was to find a good wholesaler. So I went down to the market on the intersection of Commerce Street and Jackson, which was full of merchants and jobbers selling shirts, jeans, khaki pants, caps, shoes, socks, underwear, overalls — anything you wanted.

Building up my inventory took some time. For the first few months, I used to walk into a wholesale store and purchase a few hundred dollars' worth of clothes. Several of the owners were Jewish, and I made new friends quickly. I was delighted when we could converse in Yiddish. I'd give them $100 cash, and pay the rest within 30 days. I bought whatever I could afford and began to fill up my store. My wife helped me organize the displays so that everything looked attractive.

The first few weeks, I did what I had seen my father do: I'd close up Friday and Saturday for the Sabbath and come back Monday. "That's foolish," my relatives warned me. "You won't be able to survive here like that." Well, I was hungry to make a living, so soon the little store stayed open seven days a week.

Most of my customers were African American. I quickly discovered that they had vastly different taste in clothes from the farmers and folks in Greenville, so I needed to learn what they liked. In addition to the changes in style, the sizes were a lot bigger—until then, I had never heard of a size 15EEE shoe. I was still learning English, and it also seemed many of the people in the area spoke a different dialect—"you *is*, I *ain't*, where she *be at*" —so I had to adapt to that too.

To get acquainted with the tastes of my clientele, I walked around to other stores to see what brand names and fashions were in demand. At that time it was still hard for me to read English newspapers, but I was a good viewer. I'd flip the pages to any clothing advertisements, cut them out, and that helped me decide what to sell.

Converse was a popular brand of shoes, especially among high school athletes in the area. I got to know the company's representative in Dallas, and he took a liking to me and to some other Jewish store owners, Max Biderman and Sol Prengler, who were also survivors. He offered us shoes at a 30 percent discount. Plenty of neighborhood teens began shopping in my store. In no time, I was on the map in South Dallas.

——————⟫•◦•⟪——————

When I first rented the space, there was a big sign in front for white customers and another sign in the back of the store for black customers. "Not in my store!" I said. I removed those signs. Unlike many stores at the time, black customers entered mine through the front door.

When it came to finding employees, I didn't go outside the neighborhood; I employed teenagers from Roosevelt and Lincoln High School and made a special effort to treat them nicely. At first it took me a while to get the teens adjusted.

"Whenever a new customer comes in," I told them, "you walk over and say, 'May I help you?'"

But I noticed whenever a white customer entered, they were nervous to approach him. Seeing the trepidation on their faces brought back bad memories of my youth in the ghetto, where people were constantly frightened by sadists—the feeling when you passed by a plain German solider and if he didn't like the way you looked, he'd walk over and beat you up—and I wanted no remnant of that life.

"Listen," I told them, "in this here store, everyone is equal. There is a door that goes in and out. Any customer don't like it, they can walk right out of here." If managing my store that way—resisting the more-accepted racial order of the times—meant that I would lose some business, I was prepared to close up and look for other work. Soon the kids got used to approaching all the customers.

⟫➤•०•◄⟪

In my youth, I'd often heard my father say: "If G-d gives you a new day, it can always be good. But whether it *actually* turns out to be a good or bad day will depend on you and your mindset."

Remembering those words, I applied it to my business. G-d says, "I'll send you customers, but you have to know what to do with them."

With this in mind, I also implemented certain routines for my workers. First, I always tried to make sure the young teenagers began selling in a better mood than when they arrived for work. "When it comes to selling," I would explain to them, "it's not enough just to put in effort. How you feel inside is transferred to the customers—and will influence their decisions."

Now one thing I knew was that if they were coming straight from school at 4 o'clock—on an empty stomach—it would be difficult for them to be upbeat. So I always kept a stocked refrigerator in my store to make sure they were fed well before beginning. And when I noticed one of the kids struggling, striking out with a few customers in a row, I would send him to take a break from selling, assigning him other jobs like stocking merchandise to let him unwind a bit.

I then set up incentives on a notepad for them to monitor sales and awarded a few dollars extra to the winner, less for second place, then third place. That helped overcome laziness and reluctance, but it also fueled some unhealthy competition. If one of them jumped ahead and sold to a certain customer that another eyed, for example, as soon as all customers walked out and the store was silent and empty, the next instant a surplus of curse words, n-words, and animated jive talk went flying back and forth between the angry teenagers. I let them work it out until the next customer stepped in.

"Now if you notice your customer hesitating for a while," I said, "come over and call me." So whenever one of the kids tried unsuccessfully to sell an item, I would step in. "What's the problem, sir?" I'd ask. Sometimes I'd hear, "Well, I just can't afford these." As long as I wouldn't lose money on the item, I'd gladly chip in an extra dollar or two so that a customer could come away with something from the store, especially if I noticed they badly needed shoes or the like.

In addition to building a good rapport, the ability to help people brought me tremendous personal pleasure. I was particularly sensitive to hunger — recalling the chapter in my life where I was only too happy to fetch a dirty peel from inside a sewer — and now, I was in a position to help out. I was deeply grateful to G-d for that.

CHAPTER 17
Permission

One morning shortly after I arrived in America, my uncle took me out for breakfast at the drugstore next to where he worked. In those days, a small-town drugstore also had a café. You'd tell them what you wanted, and they made milk shakes, ice cream, or hot meals, which they prepared on the spot. The clerk was a war veteran, and when he heard I was a survivor, he went to the back and brought me out some toast, eggs, and marmalade. On top of the eggs lay two crispy, crimson strips of meat.

"What are these?" I asked my uncle.

"Oh, that's *gribenes* [fried chicken skins]," he told me.

I recognized that dish — my *bubbe* had made it; my mother made them. Later I discovered it was pig's meat — bacon. With tears in my eyes, I confronted my uncle.

"Why didn't you tell me that was *hazer* [pig's meat] — it's not kosher!"

"This is Texas," he said with a chuckle. "Anything you eat down here is not going to be kosher!"

That was my first shift. Little by little, I began to change with the setting.

The next big surprise came when I needed to find a shul, a synagogue, as they referred to it here, for the High Holidays. My relatives brought me to their place of worship, the largest synagogue in Dallas. This was Reform Judaism, they told me, but I didn't yet know what that meant.

On the Sunday before the holiday, my uncle and aunt, along with my cousins, drove down to South Dallas, and they brought me to show me the synagogue. They raved about the rabbi there, his widespread community involvement and his civil rights activism. "He even has his own radio show," they told me. *Interesting, a celebrity rabbi,* I thought.

When we entered the building, two men walked over to greet us. The first was a small clean-shaven man in his 50s with a stern expression, balding in front with dark hair slicked back, and heavy black-rimmed glasses. He was dressed casually—in shorts and a white short-sleeved cotton shirt. The second gentleman was lanky, with curly hair, and looked like a businessman.

The man with glasses stuck out his hand. "Nice to meet you," he said. "I'm Rabbi Levi."

"To tell you the truth," I said, "you look more like a priest to me than a rabbi."

"Well, I *am* a rabbi," he reiterated, obviously annoyed.

"I didn't say you're not." I tried to explain, "It's just that where I come from in Poland, all the rabbis that *I* ever saw had long beards and *payos* [side curls]; they had yarmulkes on their head and wore a long *kittel* [robe]. Here, you're dressed in shorts and don't even have—"

"I understand," he interrupted. "But you're in America now, and today's Sunday. Don't worry—I'll be wearing a proper suit and tie tomorrow night at services." He turned and winked at my uncle, who returned an uncomfortable grin, clearly embarrassed by my remarks.

Then the other man, the president, interjected, "Mr. Repp, we sympathize with everything you've been through. And on behalf of the board here at Temple Emanu-El, we'd like to offer you a free membership for the next year."

I refused.

They insisted.

I explained that I had my own business and could pay a little—I didn't want to accept any charity. "Anyway," I informed them, "with my work and other obligations, you likely won't see me here except for the High Holidays."

When we left the building, after that awkward encounter, the two men likely thought I was a bit meshugah.

⸺⟫‑◦‑⟪⸺

That Tuesday evening marked Rosh Hashanah, the Jewish New Year and the beginning of the auspicious Days of Awe. In preparation for the evening service, I dressed in my finest suit and tie, and covered my head with a yarmulke. I tucked my *tallit* into a velvet bag and headed for the door.

The thought of once again stepping into a large sanctuary full of Jewish people gathered to celebrate the Jewish New Year stirred memories of quiet walks with my father through the streets of Poland, entering the grand shul in Radom, where we were welcomed by a room of glowing faces, long beards who softly murmured in Yiddish as they anticipated the evening service. The *chazzan* would take his place on the *bimah* (stand) in the center of the room to lead the congregation in prayer. Pouring out his heart, he raised the Hebrew psalms to the heavens with his strong rich voice and ancient stirring melodies. That was then. *I wonder what the atmosphere will be like in Texas,* I thought. I was keen to find out.

When we approached the Temple building, the first difference I noticed was that everyone drove to the venue in fancy cars, a far cry indeed from the way I grew up, when no one drove on the Sabbath. Then, when I went inside, I got a shock. Looking around, I was convinced we were in some kind of church: The place was filled with smooth-shaven, assimilated German Jews in fancy outfits; they all stood there stiff as a board, smoking cigarettes before the service, and the men were completely bareheaded. I was the only one wearing a yarmulke.

Then, as the service began, hymns were recited aloud in unison, slowly and robotically—in English. They even had someone playing an organ in the background. *My father would surely consider me amongst gentiles right now,* I thought.

I reflected on the little Polish *beit midrash* he would take me to during the week, where the pure and pious folk clenched their fists and tapped their chest while begging for forgiveness. With that scene in my mind, I closed my eyes and mumbled my own prayer: "Dear G-d, where are you? We lost so many fine, beautiful people in the war … As a kid, I watched your humble children; they were poor—cold, ragged, shoeless, and hungry —yet they stayed late, praying with devotion for hours in your house of study. I'm sitting here now, on this holiest day of Rosh Hashanah, listening to an organ playing—what is this?"

I doubted anybody in that room was grappling with G-d. As for me, having seen such horrors, I no longer considered myself fit to judge what was abnormal, right, or wrong. This was a different universe with a new outlook.

———❖———

As the service concluded, everyone stood up. My wife and I exchanged blessings for "a good and sweet year" with each other, and with my relatives and their friends seated close by. Then we moved through the crowd toward the exit. As we neared the door,

I glanced back and noticed the rabbi making his way through the aisle, hurrying toward us.

"That's the rabbi running toward us," I briefed my wife. "He probably wants to wish us *gut yom tov.*"

He walked up to us. "Jack, I wanted to tell you something," he said. He quickly began telling me about a committee they had put together to decide synagogue policy about skullcaps and evolving traditions. He was an educated and polished orator, but here he stumbled to get out his words — he must have repeated the phrase about a "committee" three or four times — and still, I couldn't figure out what he meant.

"Rabbi, do you have something urgent to tell me about this committee? If not, I'll bid you a good night and a sweet new year." Meanwhile, a small crowd had begun to form behind us, so he turned around and gave his attention to the eager congregants waiting to shake his hand.

The following afternoon I received a visit at my apartment from the rabbi, along with the assistant rabbi, a senior member of the synagogue, my uncle Sam, and a cousin. We all sat down, and the rabbi began again with a discussion of the board and the committees.

"Rabbi, if you recall, I told you that I'm not really interested in joining any committees."

"No, no. It's not about that," he assured me.

"Please get to the point then," I said.

Finally, he announced, "Mr. Repp, considering your past experiences, the members of our committee discussed it and we've decided that — exceptionally, in your case — we will allow you to wear your yarmulke to temple."

Mmm, I thought. This is what the free world brings — *permission* by a rabbi to wear a yarmulke.

CHAPTER 18
Hey, Greenehr

The Jews who had moved to Texas before the war were well settled. At first, it was a hard transition into the new world, especially mixing in with Southern folks, but they largely had been successful in establishing themselves. In a short time, they were making a fine living and beginning to believe they were Americans in every aspect.

They were certainly better off than their family members who'd survived the Holocaust, better off both financially and psychologically—they hadn't been through hell. We, on the other hand, were fresh out of the old country, remnants of a forgotten existence. We were less educated than they were, dressed differently, and spoke English with a heavy accent. In short, we stuck out. Of course these Americanized Jews still chatted in Yiddish, their mother tongue, but the once-fresh immigrants themselves had no compunctions about scorning the newer ones, whom they viewed as bumpkins.

Greenehr, or *griner,* is a Yiddish word that merely means "new immigrant," an adaptation of "greenhorn." But the way some Americanized Jews used that term gave me the same feeling as when I heard white people speak about "the Negroes," or other such group titles used in a demeaning way. When they saw one of us, they'd even call to you by the generic term — "Hey, *greenehr*"—rather than refer to you by name.

On Sundays, all the *greenehr* used to gather at the local Jewish Community Center, which was then on Pocahontas Street in South Dallas. There they had live music, shows, and other social events. One day, while my wife and I were talking to another couple in the crowd, I heard a voice a few feet away from me: "Hey, *greenehr*—come over here."

I slowly swung my head over my shoulder and saw a short older man, motioning for me to approach him. He was around 5 foot 6, mostly bald except for some bushy hair around his ears. I walked over.

"You looking for work?" he asked me in Yiddish.

Right away I was irked. I was a tall, slim, young gentleman, tidy and dressed in fashionable clothes. He was short and shabby, looked like a real *shlepper*—and he'd never met me. But that didn't stop him from talking to me like I was a second-class citizen.

"Mmm-hmm." I nodded. Although I'd already opened my own little store and had no intention of working elsewhere, I decided to play along and hear what he had to say.

"I have a small bakery on Forest Avenue, right across the street from the New York deli," he said. "You know where that is?" (Before Forest was renamed Martin Luther King Jr. Boulevard, the 2-mile road was one of South Dallas's largest Jewish settlements.)

"Yeah, sure I know."

"Good," he concluded, poised to take control. "I need someone to open up in the mornings, 6 a.m. sharp—to turn on the oven and start preparing everything. I'll give you $12 a week, okay?"

"Mmm-hmm."

"And I'll tell you what," he added, "you can even take home some leftover bread at the end of each day. Twice a week, I'll also give you some *Semelle* rolls. And on Fridays, for the Sabbath I'll throw in some sweet rolls." That seemed to make him feel like a true philanthropist. "All right, I'll see you on Monday morning," he said, as he patted me twice on the shoulder and walked away. I went back to join my wife in her conversation, as if nothing had happened.

Monday, as usual, I went to work at my store in South Dallas. In the late afternoon my wife was at the JCC with some friends. When that little man noticed her, he immediately marched up, hollering, "Hey — your husband didn't show up for work this morning!"

My wife was slightly taken aback. "Maybe he got lost," she replied.

"Well, tell him that if he's not there tomorrow morning on time, not to bother showing up again."

Of course, I never went there.

———⟡———

Shortly after I opened up, I began going to shows in Dallas, a merchandise mart, to stock up on clothes for my store. One day I attended a convention with a relative who had come to Dallas for the convention, and we went in a showroom. There I saw some shirts with shoulder straps and belt-like flaps that I thought would be perfect for my customers. I was excited.

But when I went to place an order, the representative said, "I don't know you. How long have you been in business?"

"One year," I answered.

He opened a book and began looking through a list. "I'm sorry," he said. "My company won't ship to you — you don't have a rating yet."

My cousin was standing near me. "Ship those to me," he said.

The rep clearly knew my cousin, who been doing business for some time. "Okay, sir, we'll send it to Sam Swartz in Greenville."

The next Sunday, my cousin was visiting Dallas. I went to pay him for the shirts he'd ordered. "Oh, those shirts?" he said. "We already sold them."

After that I realized: *A relative is a relative, but I have to look out for myself.*

⟫•◦•⟪

One of the first people I bought from was a southern Jew who went by the name "Tex." A tall, robust fellow, always impeccably dressed, Tex worked as a traveling salesman who represented a large shoe company. His company sold steel-toe shoes, sought by many of my customers employed in construction or who did any type of tough work.

Tex made sure to let me know he was doing me a favor by selling to me. "If I didn't know you're a survivor, I wouldn't waste my time selling to a little bitty store like this." Yes, he was rude and nasty.

He would glide to the front of my store in his long sleek Cadillac sedan, park his car, and stroll in holding his briefcase.

"Hey, *greenehr*, what are you buying today?" He always spoke in a belittling tone. "Go get them sizes for me," he'd bellow.

While I sped around the store counting items and checking the sizes I needed, he'd talk to me leaning back in his chair, his feet propped up on my desk, while he puffed on a fat cigar, leisurely lifting up his head between sentences to blow out rings of smoke. When he'd walk out of the store after the sale, I would feel torn up inside. *Why does he have to act that way to me?* But what could I do? I had to make a living.

Certain people enter your life at just the right time to help you take the next step. Such a man was Meyer Rachofsky. The bank I used was the Mercantile National Bank, and Meyer was the vice president of the bank. I got to know him well. When it came to financial advice, he and the bankers took me under their wing and became mentors.

Although Meyer had a reputation for being prudent when it came to loans—even to those people close to him—he really liked me. "Jack, you're going to be all right," he used to encourage me.

The first year of my business, I ran into a few surprising challenges. When my invoices arrived from a wholesaler from whom, for example, I had bought $400 worth of goods, I would pay him $200 cash. The remaining $200, he sold to another person (called a factor) at a discount. Now the invoice was payable to the third party. And that meant every $200 I owed brought an additional 4 percent for that factor. I tried to figure out a way to save on that expense, which to me seemed wasteful.

I went into the bank to speak with Meyer. "Would you do me a favor, Meyer?" I asked.

"Sure, Jack—what do you need?"

"Would you take a chance on me? I want to borrow $3,000, and the only thing I'm going to use that money for is to pay my business invoices."

From that time on, all my bills were paid within seven days. In just a short time, I moved into the first column, rated alongside all the big department stores. Now, wherever I went, people treated me better because my credit was good. That little loan from Meyer Rachofsky ended up saving me thousands—and made a respectable businessman out of me.

Shortly after my credit improved, a Lebanese man came into my store. He was a salesman from a big company in St. Louis. His company had all the same things, for better prices, that I got from Tex. That was all I needed to switch. As an added advantage, this man was respectful inasmuch as he treated me like a customer. Instead of sending me to take sizes, he'd do the work, walking around the store checking what remained and what I needed to order.

The next time Tex came to visit me, I told him I didn't need anything from him anymore. "Tex," I said, "it's been nice knowing you. At this point, you can go take out someone else's liver."

When the owner of Tex's company realized that he was no longer getting orders from me, he paid me a visit himself, along with another sales rep. "Mr. Repp, what happened? You've been a loyal customer for a while." I bit my tongue and never said a word about his employee.

When it came time to buy a house, I naturally looked to the area where the wealthy Jewish families I knew had settled. Knowing that these families sent their kids to nearby public schools, my concern was that my kids would have the same opportunity to succeed. Eventually, we found a house on Park Lane. The owner wanted $22,000. "I'll let you have it for $18,000—but I need cash," he said.

I again went to Meyer, who talked to the president from the bank, Robert Thornton. Meyer got me 3 percent interest. He handed me a check, and I bought the house. "You can pay me back a little bit at a time, but I know you are going to pay me," he said.

Owning a house in that area, we were moving up. My wife decorated the interior of our home charmingly. When we first came to America, she had a simple view of the world — after all, she was only a child when the war broke out — but she quickly developed a sophisticated taste from observation. If she came to a friend's house and saw a style of furniture she liked, it didn't take long for a similar piece to appear in our living room. Upon seeing the same item as the one in her house, her girlfriend might remark with a friendly grin: "Oh — where'd you get that?" And she'd casually reply, "Oh, Jack brought it home the other day."

Whenever my uncle and aunt came to visit Dallas from Greenville, we hosted them splendidly, with love, laughter, and good taste. In fact, they remarked how they preferred dining at our place over restaurants or their country club.

Our son David was born in 1953, and Stanley was born in 1960. We were building a family.

Now, in a tight-knit community, success can breed envy. Among our neighbors on Park Lane was another Jewish family, the Goldbergs. Our families quickly became friendly. One day I came home from work for a quick dinner, and found the house empty — *must be at the Goldbergs's*, I figured. So I walked over to their house.

Sure enough, my family was there. Now Mrs. Goldberg was a heavy woman; she must have weighed around 350 pounds. She also liked to talk a lot and wasn't afraid to speak her mind. Lying in her usual place on the sofa, she called me over. "Hey, Jack, I want to speak to you for a second. Now, I'm going to ask you a question — and you tell me the truth!"

"I don't owe you any money, so why should I lie to you?" I joked.

"Our husbands travel all week long to make a living. You stay here in Dallas."

"Yes," I said.

"Tell me something," she continued, "how in the world do you damn immigrants come down here, you buy a house, you own a store, a car—where do you all get that money?"

Mrs. Blanc, the neighbor across the street, was there in the room, and she chimed in. "Yeah, tell me too. I also wondered about that," she said.

Now I had two hawks on my case. I figured I could kill them both in one shot, so I leaned over to Mrs. Goldberg, and very gently I said: "Mrs. Goldberg, you are so right. We refugees came here with nothing. But, you see, there's a place called the Hebrew Free Loan Association in Dallas. They give us each $25,000, with 20 years to repay it." (In truth, $250 was likely the most you could borrow at that time.)

I said goodbye and left them in envy to chew on my tale. I heard there were quite a few phone calls that night in the community—"You know what kind of funding those damn *greenehr* are receiving?"

CHAPTER 19

My Own Holiday

When previously black neighborhoods were demolished for factories and stores, the residents migrated to South Dallas. As the African Americans continued to move into the neighborhood, most white families packed up and moved out. By the mid-1950s, the hub of Jewish life changed from South to North Dallas. Businesses closed; Jewish synagogues and organizations followed their congregants and relocated. A once tight-knit Jewish community in South Dallas slowly unraveled and disappeared.

Then the crime rate in South Dallas began to increase, and the neighborhood became more and more dangerous. Almost all Jewish merchants retired or reopened their businesses in another part of town. "You need to get out of there," our friends warned me. But I stood firm. I kept my store in South Dallas.

My store was always open from early in the morning to late at night. My competitors closed at 6 in the evening. Sometimes I stayed till 10. If anybody needed a pair of socks or a pair of gloves or maybe a pair of tennis shoes, I was there.

It was late one night, the security guard had left a few hours earlier, and I was getting ready to close up and come home when a customer walked in. He quickly approached me.

"May I help you?" I asked.

He lifted his hand and was pointing a gun at me. "Give me your money or I kill you."

Now, ever since I arrived in America, I had enjoyed watching *The Three Stooges* on television. I don't remember exactly what I was thinking at that moment—I must have been foolish—but I figured he was playing with me.

"You got your gun," I told him, imitating Moe's snarky voice, "I'm gonna go get my broom handle." I walked back a few steps behind the counter, pretending to search for it.

"I ain't playing around," the man yelled, shaking his pistol in short jittery movements.

"I ain't playing around either—you imbecile!" I snarled, still in character.

We went back and forth a few times, and then stood still, face to face, silently staring into each other's eyes.

After a few seconds, he shook his head. "Man, you crazy!" he said with a smile, turned around, and hurried out the door. Once again, G-d watched over me.

<hr />

Fellow store owners kept telling me that I needed to purchase insurance. I created my own insurance: I hired a tall, sturdy black man by the name of James Wallace who weighed around 365 pounds. I had a security outfit made for him and gave him a sidekick.

Then they advised me that I needed an alarm system during the night. Instead I put up a sign in the window that said, "Beware of Bear." That seemed to work. Sometimes, as I walked by, I'd overhear someone on the street whispering to his friend, "See that dude—keeps a bear in his store." Then someone in the area apparently reported me for animal cruelty, or not having a license.

During that time, there was a lot of theft, which led to some nasty confrontations. One Jewish store owner, upon catching someone shoplifting a pair of socks, ran after the customer and chased him down the street. The crook got nervous, turned around, and shot him dead on the street. Others had suffered retribution after reporting someone to the police. When I heard about those incidents, I said to myself, *I was not born with any material possessions, and when I leave this world, I'm not taking anything with me but a shroud. Nothing that small is worth dying for!*

To be sure, we sometimes caught people stealing. Every so often, a customer would walk in, take several pairs of pants into the dressing room to try on, and then come out with only two.

If I noticed it, I never confronted the person or had them arrested. Rather, after he got through paying, I'd casually remark, "Sir, when you went to change, you must have forgotten to take off a pair of pants underneath."

"Oh, no, I ain't trying to steal—"

"Just keep it on," I'd say. "You can pay for it another time."

Next Friday, the same customer would return. This time, however, the first thing that came out of his mouth was "Mr. Jack, I ain't going to steal nothing in your store."

Even today, I meet people who appreciate that gesture. "Mr. Jack, you know, I'm so thankful to you. You could've given me a record for the rest of my life. But you didn't say nothing, didn't call no police on me. I have a family now, grandchildren and all…"

⟫•◦•⟪

The way I saw it, if you know you're going to be living around thieves, you have to have common sense. I got to know the people in the neighborhood. If a recognized member of the Black Panthers or community leader walked in to buy something, I'd wrap up his purchase and also hand him a gift. A little bit of goodness can go a long way: Once, when there was violence on the streets during turbulent times, a teenager picked up a bottle and moved to throw it through my window. Three men in the neighborhood immediately stood in front — "Don't you dare," they warned him. "This is our store!"

It wasn't a calculation; I think people understood that I didn't open up my store there just to take. And one should always give more than one takes. More notably, I believe that I survived down there for one reason — I lived the right way, the way my parents had shown me. Throughout my childhood, I heard my parents say, "If you are hungry, I'm going to feed you. If you are cold, I'm going to put something on your back."

Therefore, if I noticed someone walking into my store barefoot or with torn shoes, and after trying on a new pair, they realized that they only had $6 cash — the shoes in those days were $8.99 — I'd tell them, "Keep the shoes on." I took whatever they could afford to pay. "You don't owe me anything," I said, "just whenever you pass by, if you have 50 cents or a dollar on you, bring it in."

You see, most people who came into my store were living in extreme poverty. And I tried to help them out as much as possible. Reverend Willie Jones, for example, was a Baptist preacher who lived on Canal Street. He had 13 kids, and his wife had to stay home to care for them. All his income was from the little church, and the salary he received was meager.

Reverend Jones used to pull up to my store in his old station wagon and walk into the store with some of his children. Oftentimes, they didn't have the cash to pay for clothes, so I'd take out some bills from my pocket, or give him some items on credit.

"You a real blessing to us, Mr. Jack," he'd say.

With these small acts, I was able to build a good rapport with the African American community. Everyone in the neighborhood knew me. They showed my family respect. In fact, when my wife pulled up in front of the store, people on the street often ran just to open the door for her. That made me proud. Occasionally, parents of my employees used to pick up my children and take them home to play with their kids. We'd also invite their kids for sleepovers, and they'd lie side by side with my kids. July 4 and other national holidays, during which my store stayed open, resident families used to walk in and bring me food.

I stayed in that area for 18 years, until I expanded and opened Repp's Department Store on Second Avenue near Fair Park at Hatcher Street. In that 8,000-square-foot store, we sold items ranging from diapers, children's clothes, men's and ladies' apparel, lingerie, handbags, luggage, shoes, hats, and more.

⎯⎯⎯◦⎯⎯⎯

Every day, when I woke up, put on a suit, and went to my store, I focused on one thing: I wanted my wife and three children to be no less than anyone else around, to be able to do all the same things as other people, to do everything that other children at their school did.

As business grew, if I knew my family was financially secure —that we had a good home and that my kids went to good schools and didn't lack any necessities—I had confidence we'd all be okay. The sight of my wife driving the kids to Kip's restaurant down the street, treating our children and their friends and having a good time, and then in later years my daughter, Lotty, coming home from college for winter break and hosting a group of her sorority sisters—these little things brought me joy. I didn't mind the expenses — it did me good. It kept me working hard and gave me something to live for.

I worked seven days a week and never took a vacation. My summer vacations consisted of closing the store for a few hours. Sometimes, when I took the afternoon off, I put up a sign in the window that read: "Religious holiday — back at 5:15." I stopped by the deli shop, bought some rolls, salami, and salads, and then joined my wife and kids at the local Jewish Community Center to swim, sit outside, and have a family picnic. To me, that was a lovely vacation.

I soon discovered that a few of my business competitors, other Jews, didn't care for that sign in the window. They approached the rabbi — "What religious holiday is it today?" they asked. When they heard it was an ordinary day, they assumed "That *greenehr* must be up to no good."

I found out because the rabbi came to me, asking, "Jack, was there a holiday this week that I don't know about?"

I ignored the complaints. After what I'd been through in my life — the darkest darkness — I figured I was entitled to proclaim my own holiday once in a while.

CHAPTER 20
No Longer a Hidden Book

How much of what a person ends up with is a result of one's achievements, and how much was received? I'd say most of what we end up with is a blessing from above.

At a Passover seder, recounting the deliverance of our ancestors from the brutal Egyptian exile, we come to a passage that reads: "Our ancestors were slaves unto Pharaoh." Well, in my eyes, what I saw in the death camps was worse than slavery. I have undergone torture and torment, much of which I didn't mention in these pages. I've seen sadists cut people's tongues and ears off; they took away your shoes in the icy winter. For years you never saw a bed. You slept on a wooden shelf with 20 bodies, unable to even turn your head. We were treated worse than animals.

Reflecting on past pain from a more removed perspective, I reckon anyone who withstood what we did must have had steel reserves inside. It's a wonder to me that you find a Holocaust survivor today who managed to stay sane and to live a normal life —finding a spouse, buying a house, having children and grandchildren. I certainly never thought I would see anything like that. And in the end, G-d gave me life, something that millions of others around me didn't get. I managed to live comfortably, build a family, and run my own business for over 40 years.

With all that, there was one thing that always bothered me. Among friends at social gatherings, I would hear people recollecting their youth in America: proms, drive-in movies, glory days

Me, 1958.

From left: Stanley, David, Edna, me, and Lotty.

Me and Edna.

in college filled with honky-tonk, fraternity memberships, and classic football games. I would listen with envy. I felt ashamed. I had none of those experiences, and I felt as if I missed out on a chunk of life, that I was robbed of the chance to receive an education, cut short at the age of 16.

My Sarah, whom I met in 1998, two years after my wife, Edna, passed away, put an end to all that thinking. "Tell me," she said. "Who's better off? Those professionals, with their degrees, or you, with your good common sense?" She pounded her encouragement into me. "What you have been through and accomplished in your time," she told me, "is worth more than any academic education!"

Sarah grew up in Tyler, Texas, and we had both been previously married 50 years before being introduced by our children, who knew each other from Temple Emanu-El. One day after services, I said to her, "May I walk you to your car?"—and we've been together ever since.

From the onset of our relationship, Sarah encouraged me to speak publicly about my story, saying that with my memory and personality, I could make a difference. "You have something valuable to share," she said. "You should be telling your story to all these other people—and to the schoolchildren in particular."

So I began what amounted to a second career, traveling around, retelling many of the nightmares I've experienced, things I had never discussed. As time consuming and exhausting as it sometimes was to lecture and emotionally revive these experiences, I have never taken money for any speaking engagement, which in my view would be like blood money.

Sarah handles, and continues to manage, all the logistics of my lectures. We are now both in our 90s, but whenever a group wants me to speak, I'll be there, sometimes the next day—

speaking to adults at synagogues, schoolchildren in classrooms, university students, diverse visitors at the local Holocaust Museum, or audiences in remote Texas towns. I consider telling my story part of my purpose—to make sure that others remember.

Engaging an audience with my story is also fulfilling. My life is no longer a hidden book. I'm not afraid to open up anymore. It continually amazes me when, after a lecture, I see adults lining up to ask me questions, coming over to share their impressions, or to simply give me a hug. Often a person will confide, "You know, my great-grandmother was Jewish." That lets me know that my words have touched them.

I never thought we would witness anti-Semitism and white supremacy resurfacing like they have today, more than 70 years after I was liberated. And since we unfortunately still find humans of this caliber, America needs to be conscientious about it. A raging blaze doesn't suddenly start. There are always little sparks and fires, but if you can snuff them out before they spread, you have accomplished something. Being vigilant, not apathetic, is part of my message.

The freedom we enjoy here in America, and too easily take for granted, comes with the responsibility to envisage the past. That's one of the reasons I've spent the last two decades speaking out and being an active member of the Dallas Holocaust Museum/Center for Education and Tolerance.

On the flip side, as I drive around Dallas, Texas, I see thriving Jewish populations. Each synagogue looks like a palace. Temple Emanu-El, the place where I've been a member for more than 60 years, has evolved since I arrived: Now rabbi and congregants alike proudly don a yarmulke and *tallit*. There are ongoing Torah classes and thousands of members. Whenever I manage to attend prayer services, and the passage of mourner's *kaddish* is

Sarah and me (courtesy of Dallas Holocaust Museam).

Speaking at the Dallas Holocaust Museum, the International Day of Peace,
September 2015 (courtesy of KTVT-TV).

recited—the prayer for departed souls—I don't just stand and honor my parents. I say that prayer for the six million men, women, and children murdered, knowing that many don't have any descendants.

The community in general has blossomed. I've recently been invited to traditional Shabbat meals at private homes, watched schoolchildren at the table proudly singing blessings in Hebrew, and therein I've discovered a resurgence of my sweet childhood.

—————

Once upon a time, in the depths of hell, I had a dream and I had a jealousy. I fantasized about the day I could eat one loaf of bread. I was jealous of that butterfly that flew away from a Nazi's boot while I couldn't move anywhere. Today, thanks to the Almighty, I have fulfilled that dream and jealousy in great measure. I received more from life than I ever thought—a loving wife, a nice house, sent my children to good schools and universities, traveled the world, and watched grandchildren grow. And like my father, I operated my own business and was able to help people.

But the pain of the past remains fresh. Every night, before lying down to sleep, I kiss the picture of my parents. I remember all their lessons. When I sit down for Friday night dinner I never touch my food before my Sarah eats, just as my father did. You see, in a lifetime, G-d gives and G-d takes—and he gave me a lot too.

I always say: You have to take the good with the bad, mix it up, and make it all good.

Gainesville, Texas, May 2017.

The production of this memoir was made possible through
the generous sponsors listed here, in loving memory of the following:

——⟫•◦•⟪——

Lillian and Larry Beck (by Jarrod and Shiva Beck)

Esther and Ben Bialosky (anonymously)

Leslie and Ann Blecher (by Shane and Tracey Stein)

Jack Brickman (by Shane and Tracey Stein)

Emma and Ben Josin (by Sherry and Kenny Goldberg)

Karl Krause (anonymously)

Idel, Jusha, and Ted Kremer (by George and Ilone Kremer)

Max and Sonya Mann (by Brian Leftin)

Paula Olenberg (by Stuart and Sheryl Wernick)

Shlomit Olshansky (by Igor and Liya Olshansky)

Sidney and Esther Stein (by Shane and Tracey Stein)

Laura and Morris Rabinowitz by (Jarrod and Shiva Beck)

Phil and Hannah Rosenthal (by Shane and Tracey Stein)

Sonia Tessler (by Reesa and David Feinstein)

Rachel, Emanuel, and Ron Zahler (anonymously)

For all the beautiful souls lost in the Holocaust (by Andy Schultz)

——⟫•◦•⟪——

56335290R00090

Made in the USA
Columbia, SC
23 April 2019